Going South

Going South:
An Antarctic Experience

John M. Reynolds

Marshall Pickering

All photographs remain the copyright of John M. Reynolds.

Marshall Morgan and Scott
Marshall Pickering
3 Beggarwood Lane, Basingstoke, Hants RG23 7LP, UK

Copyright © 1986 by John Reynolds
First published in 1986 by Marshall Morgan and Scott Publications Ltd
Part of the Marshall Pickering Holdings Group
A subsidiary of the Zondervan Corporation

All rights reserved. No part of this publication may be reproduced, stored in a retrieval system, or transmitted, in any form or by any means, electronic, mechanical, photocopying, recording or otherwise, without the prior permission in writing, of the publisher

British Library CIP Data

Reynolds, John
  Going south : an Antarctic experience.
  1. Christian life
  I. Title
  248.4   BV4501.2

ISBN 0 551 01376 1

Text set in Plantin by
Brian Robinson, Buckingham
Printed in Great Britain by Anchor Brendon Ltd, Tiptree, Essex.

Contents

	Preface	7
1:	Southward Ho!	9
2:	All at Sea, Icebergs and Hope	18
3:	To First Base	30
4:	Christmas	41
5:	The Sound of Ice	60
6:	The Goodenough Camp	79
7:	Towards Eternity	98
8:	Faith, Hope and Charity	112
9:	Return of the Wanderers	123
10:	The Rescue	134
11:	Stanley and Friends	141
12:	Shackleton's Island	150
13:	The Tonsberg Bells	163
14:	Homecoming	172
15:	The Aftermath	180
	Glossary	182
	Map 1: Approximate routes taken to and from the Antarctic	188
	Map 2: Routes taken whilst in the Antarctic Peninsula	189

Preface

This book is an account of what it is like for a single man in his early twenties to go to Antarctica for six months. It is based on two seasons in the Antarctic Peninsula which have been amalgamated into one for the purpose of the story. Consequently, many of the events are not in their correct historical order. The material is based on four volumes of my personal diaries and extracted from letters sent to friends and family who have very kindly loaned them back to me during the writing of this book. However, the total experience of visiting Antarctica is indelibly etched into my memory and undoubtedly has had a profound effect on me as a person. Hopefully the style of the book reflects that. All the events described are true and all the characters are real or based on real people but some names have been changed. This book is not about any particularly great or historic voyage or about a notable or famous person. It is just the opposite, an account of how an ordinary person went to Antarctica to do a job of work and, more importantly, how that voyage affected me physically, emotionally and spiritually. No one can go to Antarctica and not be affected by it. I had never been so cold for so long before, neither had I been so frightened as I was on several occasions. Also I learned a vast amount about myself in that isolation and so this book traces parts of my own journey into myself.

I hope that people who read this will not only learn something about what it is like to work in Antarctica, but also will identify with some of the personal, moral, emotional and spiritual issues raised, and God willing, be helped.

The actual journeys south took place over the Austral summers of 1978–79 and 1979–80, before the violent and bloody war with Argentina over the Falkland Islands. Although the character of the islands has been irreversibly altered by the presence of a dramatically increased garrison, civilian life continues much as before. In contrast, Grytviken on South Georgia will never be the same again, and the account of life there is of a past era.

None of the events described in this book would have been possible without the tremendous support of my colleagues and friends of the British Antarctic Survey. To all of them I give my thanks. In addition several have kindly read through the manuscript of the book and their comments are greatly appreciated. Similarly, my dear friend Sue who features prominently in the following pages was also gracious enough to read a draft. Her support in this project has been marvellous. Last but by no means least, I must thank my wife Moira for her valiant proof reading and comments as she has read every word I have written more times than she would care to remember, and supported and encouraged me throughout the entire project.

Note:

Words marked with an asterisk are explained in the Glossary.
See also the maps provided on pp. 188–189, giving clear detail of the exact routes covered in the expedition.

1: Southward Ho!

Terminal Three at Heathrow airport is a very impersonal place. With all the keen anticipation and excitement of finally leaving for Antarctica, it was good to meet up in the departure lounge with my colleagues from the British Antarctic Survey. We were all looking forward to our trip south. Thoughts of family and friends to whom we had just said goodbye were displaced by the immediacy of our departure. About 1 pm we were jammed into a Pan Am Jumbo 747 flight bound for J. F. Kennedy airport, New York. The giant aircraft rumbled along to the runway and then took off smoothly, climbing into the haze and clouds to its cruising altitude of 34,000 feet. Our pilot, Captain Johnson, informed us of the weather at New York – snow, drizzle and 0°C, somewhat worse than London, but very tame relative to what we were to encounter in Antarctica. Our flight time was longer than the seven hours expected because of considerable head winds. Our descent to New York was long and tedious as well as being uncomfortably bumpy due to turbulence. However, we touched down safely and taxied into the terminal area. We had been on the aircraft for nearly nine hours. Inside the airport buildings we had the rigmarole of passing through immigration. Manning the passport control desk was a very terse and unfriendly immigration officer.

'What yer doin' here?' he asked gruffly.

'I'm in transit to Antarctica,' I replied.

'Oh yeah? And I'm John Wayne.'

I could see that this was going to be one of those nights.

After further explanation, I was nodded through. When a couple of colleagues met the same officer and presumably said more or less the same as me, he just looked at them disbelievingly and let them through with no further ado. We were then let loose on the facilities of J. F. Kennedy airport for transit passengers. At 8 pm local time (1 am GMT), feeling somewhat jaded, we dawdled along to Gate 6 in readiness to embark on our flight to Montevideo, Uruguay. About three hours into our flight we were served with a very large meal. This was followed by a film whose title might have described the food – *Grease* – starring Olivia Newton John, an old favourite of mine. At about 6 am I tried to doze off but to no avail as we entered some clear air turbulence which shook us around for a while. As I was fortunate enough to have a window seat, I popped up the blind and peered out. Beneath us I could see a hazy green forest, part of the Amazon jungle, but what was most impressive was the sky. Spreading as far as the horizon was a canvas of brilliant colours, bright reds and yellows, with pinpricks of sparkling stars which gradually faded into the lightening blue of a most memorable dawn. Finally, after ten and a half hours on the plane we were even more relieved to disembark at Rio than we were at New York. Our faces began to look haggard and our bodies ached from sitting for so long. We were only given about forty minutes at Rio, just time enough to drink some real Brazilian coffee and buy a couple of postcards before having to re-embark. By this time I was really wearying of flying. The novelty of it all had quickly faded. I decided that I would not like to have to fly on long-haul routes regularly; there seemed to be nothing less glamorous. The insides of aircraft are very much of a muchness. Standing in long queues in impersonal airports at all hours of the day and night, having to deal with officials of all tempers and degrees of honesty, often tangling with languages with which one was not familiar, soon removed any possible romance or glamour.

We were not allowed to leave the aircraft in Buenos Aires so we had to wait patiently inside until we could leave for our final destination, Montevideo. This last leg across the Mar del Plata took only forty minutes. On arrival, we were through customs and immigration in no time. This was in part due to the fact that when we transferred aircraft in New York en route to Montevideo our luggage had stayed on board and was now in Houston, Texas! We were met at the airport by our agent whose job it was to smooth our passage through the official channels. We were to stay in Monte for a couple of days until the BAS research ship RRS *Bransfield* arrived. It gave us a couple of days to unwind from the 25 hours or so of being cooped up in an aircraft. It also gave us the opportunity of seeing a little of Uruguay while we waited for our luggage.

Next morning, after a leisurely continental breakfast, Jerry, a fellow glaciologist, and I then decided to stroll into town to do some sightseeing. It was not yet 10 am but the air temperature was well up into the 70s Fahrenheit. Montevideo was a curious mixture of building styles but all appeared to be variations of Spanish architecture. There were tall crumbling facades with washing unfurled across the narrow streets between opposite balconies. The streets were dusty and grimy and the slight breeze puffed litter along the broken pavements. Stray dogs sniffed and pawed at the strewn rubbish which gave rise to a very distinctive aroma. We eventually arrived at a palace-like building. Jerry and I climbed the massive flight of granite steps up to the columned entrance which appeared to be shut. I peered through the glass door and saw a grey uniformed man who then opened the door and invited us in. Any fears that we might have had about being arrested for trespassing on government property had long gone. This man was one of the official keepers of their Houses of Parliament. As it was during the summer recess, we were treated to a personal guided tour of the whole place, even inside both chambers of parliament, the Uruguayan equivalents of the House of

Commons and House of Lords. Our guide was obviously proud of his charge and enthusiastically explained in Spanish which great artists had painted the magnificent oils in the various galleries, and then outlined the styles of architecture in each area of the building. There were fantastic facades of polished marble and granite with a curious blend of Byzantine, Graeco-Roman, Pompeiian and several other styles of interior decoration in which gold leaf featured very prominently. We were shown what was, according to our guide, the longest palace hall in the whole of South America.

Unfortunately, we had to leave to return to our hotel by noon to try to resolve the practical problem of our missing luggage. However, there was still no news of it and consequently we felt anxious and frustrated. All we were told was that we ought to visit the Pan Am office in town, which we did straight away. Four of us went in to see the counter clerk to whom we explained our situation. The Uruguayan woman behind the desk listened to our plight then cutely shrugged her shoulders and said, 'Eh, why worry senores, it 'appens all ze time!' We felt that this really did not help the situation even if it had been some comfort to know that we were not alone in our plight. The office manager told us that our baggage had been returned from Houston to New York and then flown on south to Montevideo, so we had to go to the airport at once to clear everything through customs. My case had been irreparably damaged but at least everything was there. Next day was free as the BAS ship *Bransfield* was not due into port for another 24 hours. Four of us had booked to go on a coach tour to Punte del Este, reputedly the best known resort in South America. It was situated at the junction of the Mar del Plata and the Atlantic Ocean, east of Montevideo. On arriving, we headed straight for the beach where we body-surfed in the Atlantic and sunbathed. The beach, despite its size and the heat of the day, was deserted. We were very fortunate to be lazing under the tropical sun. After all, many people spent a fortune to holiday there and yet we were being paid for our pleasure. After three hours or so on the beach we rejoined the coach for a tour of the resort. We visited the millionaires' quarter where avenues of palm trees were flanked by manicured lawns watered by underground irrigators, and whose lush green grass contrasted with the shrivelled brown vegetation seen everywhere else. The villas themselves were immaculate with bright whitewashed walls and cream coloured thatch. We were not surprised to learn that the average price of these mansions was around a quarter of a million pounds. We drove on to see where the rich moored their large and expensive yachts and launches, then turned back towards the Uruguayan capital.

Back in our hotel some hours later I showered off the heat of the day, the cold water appeasing the tingling of my sunburnt skin; I looked like a medium done beef steak. Feeling relaxed after what had been a very enjoyable day I was ready to do justice to a good South American dinner. Afterwards I retired to my room to write my diary and some letters. I sat at a little table close by the open window so I could look at the view over the river and watch the ever-changing sunset. Fronds of palm trees along the river bank swayed gently in the breeze. Street lights flickered on as night advanced and the orange ball of the sun sank below the horizon. Sitting alone in my room accentuated the fact that although I had enjoyed the day and was continuing to appreciate the tropical evening, it would have been even better to have shared the experience with someone, a special friend. I almost felt a prisoner to my job in that I had no option but to be there. I had no control over my circumstances. I was obliged to stay in Uruguay, away from friends and family. It made sitting there like a self-inflicted solitary confinement; after all I had consciously wanted to go south and knew in my mind what that entailed. I was now finding out the implications of that decision with my heart. It was not that I wanted to go home. Far from it. I would have rather had my friends join me so they too could experience what I had been fortunate enough to sample. It was as if I had been saturated with the experiences. It was a very deeply-felt emotion, almost an ache. So as the sun set, I thought of Sue and how much she would have liked to have watched that same view. I went out to the balcony railings and breathed in deeply, taking into myself more of the beauty of the scene. The sensation was very satisfying; it had been a good day and I thanked God for it.

Next morning, we had to vacate our rooms as we were due to embark upon RRS *Bransfield* which had sailed into port during the night. I was eager to see what she was like. When our agent met us at the hotel to take us to the port, he told us that a case of hepatitis had been confirmed on board ship and thus she was quarantined until everyone had had a vaccination. By mid-morning we were at the water's edge and I could see *Bransfield* moored out in the middle of the bay. Despite her small size, her bright red hull and white superstructure made her very conspicuous against the grey water and the dull overcast sky. A liberty launch picked us up from the jetty and took us to the ship. We lugged our baggage along the shaky stairway up the side of the hull to the main deck, then up a steep flight of steps to the expedition deck where we found our cabins. Before we were permitted to unpack and sort out our gear we had to report to the sickbay. The ship's doctor was waiting for us with his needle. I have always hated vaccinations and there had been nasty rumours as to how large the needle was going to be. One of the men had fainted at just the sight of it! Soon it was my turn, and then, before I knew it, it was all over; the injection had not been as bad as I had anticipated. However, I had not reckoned on the after-effects. Within an hour or so, everyone on board ship seemed to be walking around with a slight limp or sitting very carefully on one cheek!

After lunch, Howard, a technician, Jerry, Julian (my boss) and I went by launch back to Montevideo to spend the rest of the day ashore. After wandering around for a while, we came across a cinema which was showing an English film with Spanish sub-titles. The film projector broke down four times and occasionally the film went askew; the sound was turned down so as not to detract from the sub-titles. Somehow that cinema epitomised the flavour of Montevideo. When we left the cinema it was pouring with rain in true tropical style. All was quiet except for the passing of a few old cars and the banter of people in tiny wine bars. We had to pass through the 'red light' area to reach the quayside we required. Fortunately the prostitutes stayed inside the bistros giggling amongst themselves and occasionally called out to us in Spanish and beckoned. We reached the quayside and caught the midnight launch back to *Bransfield*. My sunburn from the time at Punte del Este allowed me to sleep only fitfully so I was grateful to be able to laze around on board ship throughout the following morning. The port of Montevideo was quite busy with many small craft plying to and fro between a couple of larger ships, tankers and cargo vessels. *Bransfield* was visited by a small launch which tried to sell fresh groceries. The swarthy men on board shifted heavy boxes of fruit and vegetables with consummate ease. In the heat of the day they were stripped down to greasy vests or completely to the waist, showing off their bronzed skin. Even though we were becoming tanned by the sun we all still looked very pale in comparison. That afternoon, Howard, Jerry and I caught a bus to Cerro, a military museum housed in an old castle which was not elaborate but was kept reasonably well and we passed an interesting couple of hours there. The weather was deteriorating and the sky was overcast and squally. The air temperature had dropped and offered us some relief from the more usual humid heat that we had been experiencing. That evening, we decided to stay on board ship and spend a quiet evening chatting and playing darts in the fiddery*. We discussed the day's events and also our plans for the following day. Howard, Julian and I thought it would be good to try to attend an early morning service at the Church of England cathedral. At 6.30 am that Sunday morning we caught the launch to town and then walked to the cathedral only to find its imposing doors firmly locked. There was no notice outside to indicate when the services were to be held so we walked to the hotel in which we had stayed when we first arrived in Monte and had some coffee. On our way back towards the cathedral we saw some people going inside. We asked someone when the morning service was but it transpired that it was too late for us to be able to attend. My first Sunday away and no church service. It felt odd and I was disappointed. I thought of my friends in the church at Bromley and how they would be enjoying a lively challenging service. I thought of how Sue would be singing with the youth choir 'Revelation' in which I used to sing.

Just after 11 am we were on our way south again, this time bound for Port Stanley in the Falkland Islands. As we steamed out of the harbour, thoughts of what I had seen in Monte crossed my mind. The city seemed odd and full of contrasts; there were many magnificent grand buildings but so many more in disrepair. It was a city in a time warp as it gave the impression it was still back in the 1930s. Old cars such as Model-T Fords stood side by side with dishevelled more recent vehicles. The coaches on which we had travelled were literally falling apart, and were held together in places only by string and chewing gum. The passengers were as varied as the vehicles on which they travelled; apart from people, there might be a goat or a piglet being taken to market and being held in someone's arms to stop it from running loose. In the streets, shoeless ninos held out their grubby little hands, cocking their heads to one side and begging pathetically for money; old widows dressed in black tried to sell individual aspirins in the market, ever persistent with their toothless grins and wrinkled faces. Old men with white stubble on their weather-beaten faces sat in dark doorways aimlessly watching the world go by. It made me feel uneasy. To these people we must have seemed very rich, with our smart clothes, and our cameras slung around our necks. It made me wonder about the real value of life, why there should be such squalor on so large a scale. There was a great deal of money evident at Punte del Este, and enormous wealth was obvious within the Palace and similar buildings. It was sad to think that with raging inflation in their economy the situation was going to worsen. Why would a God of love allow this imbalance between the rich and the poor with all the attendant suffering? I had no ready answers.

2: All at Sea, Icebergs and Hope

Life on board ship was quite pleasant. I was sharing a cabin with three others, Jerry, Derek (the dentist), and Dougy (King Fid* and diver). Our cabin was on the port side two decks below the bridge. Although not large enough to swing a cat, there was adequate room for the four of us. There were two sets of two tiered bunks on either side of the cabin, a wash basin and a writing desk. Beneath the porthole a bench seat provided more room to spread out. Our kit was jammed into wardrobes at the other end of the bunks or the drawer beneath the bottom bunks. The individual berths could be screened from the rest of the cabin by curtains so allowing some privacy. All our facilities were on the one deck. The Fiddery, up for'd, provided recreational space — bar, library, radio, tape deck and film screen — and was the main community room. The scradge palace* was at the aft end of the deck and consisted of the gash* area where the food was hoisted from the galley on the deck below, and then dished out cafeteria style to the Fids*. Meals were eaten seated at long tables with storm battens at the edges which could be fixed to stop plates etc., sliding off the table during rough weather. On the aft wall was a large nautical map of both the north and south Atlantic; a transparent perspex cover allowed the ship's route to be marked on daily in wax crayon so we could monitor our progress. The main trouble with shipboard life was not having much to do to occupy one's time. Our trip to the Falklands would only take us four days or so, so there was no particular trouble, but on longer journeys it was to play a more important role in people's psyche. My cabin mates and I coped well together. Jerry and I had shared an office back in Cambridge so we knew each other reasonably well whereas I had never met either of the other two prior to embarking at Montevideo. Many of the Fids on board had sailed all the way from Southampton together and had become acquainted en route. Those of us who joined ship at Monte had to establish ourselves within an already developed community. Opportunities to meet everyone else decreased the further south we sailed as the seas became rougher and so folk felt less well and stayed in their bunks for most of the time; I was no exception, not being the best of sailors and it took me several days to acquire my sea legs. As I spent much of my time in those first few days on my bunk I had plenty of time to read, to think and to chat with my cabin mates if they were around. In conversation the subject of Christianity came up and I discovered that Derek was a regular attender of services at his local parish church in Yorkshire. Jerry and Dougy were both uninterested in God-talk. However, they never ribbed me about my quiet time which surprised and relieved me. Jerry did pull my leg occasionally about religion as he had the the previous Sunday in Monte. When after finding that there was no suitable service at the Eclesia Inglesa, Jerry had quipped, 'What's showing at the other places?' Christianity was not a subject close to the heart of most Fids and I soon realised that I was not likely to have much Christian fellowship during my time south. That in itself posed two issues. First, I had to be as self-sufficient as I could be in human terms to sustain my Christian faith, and secondly, I had to try to do my best to be a good witness to those around me. I knew that although I was being supported in prayer by friends back in England, I was still on my own on this trip.

Food on board ship was both plentiful and on the whole good quality. In the tropics, I found that I ate less because of the heat, but I drank much more to avoid dehydration. As we sailed further south so the temperature dropped and I ate more and drank less. I had no real worry about putting on weight at this time as the roughness of the sea, especially for the first couple of days, caused me to lose many of my meals. I looked forward immensely to calmer waters. On our second day out of Monte, I was assigned to a working party. Our first job was to scrub the decks with a special detergent mixed with a liberal sprinkling of sand. It was not particularly hard work and it enabled us to be actively employed out on deck in the fresh air and sunshine. The weather was fine and warm and most of us wore just shorts and a tee-shirt when working outside.

After the day's work was done, there was still plenty of time to wander around on deck to look at the scenery and watch the birds. Even though we were hundreds of miles from land, there were dozens of birds trailing the ship, flying across the stern hunting for scraps of food. It was remarkable how these birds seemed to glide for such large distances and so close to the wave tops without flapping their wings. What did disappoint me was the number of small oil patches we came across right in the middle of the south Atlantic. The unwanted vestiges of man seemed to reach everywhere.

One thing surprised me about myself; living within an all-male community was not as perturbing as I had imagined it would be. I did not feel that I had missed Sue more than if I had been in a normal balanced community back in England. I thought I would have felt more isolated from her than I did. Yet it was not that my feelings for her were not great, but it was as if, in my own mind, I knew that I need not worry about our relationship until my return. I was psychologically adjusting myself to the emotional separation. It was easy to think like that at this early stage of the expedition, but would it be so easy later on? I very much looked forward to receiving a letter from her to learn how she was faring during my absence.

The remainder of the voyage to Port Stanley was spent reading, writing letters, postcards and my diary – when the weather was calm enough. The evenings were spent in idle conversation whilst supping a glass or two of port. We had one day of bad weather and I had the misfortune to be on gash* duty. I felt awful, especially whilst cleaning out the slops bucket. At one point during dinner the ship suddenly lurched 15 degrees sending food, dishes and people everywhere. A loud cheer went up from the scradge palace when the Fids saw and heard everything go flying. Remarkably, only one plate and a salad dressing bottle were broken. That evening, having completed all my chores after a mammoth meal which must have involved all the crockery on the ship judging from the amount of washing up I had to do, the Falkland Islands were sighted. Rock-hopper penguins porpoised along beside the ship as we neared the narrows leading to the port. Gradually we entered the channel near Pembroke Point with its lighthouse, and a few moments later, Port Stanley came into view tucked into the side of a low hill. After a while it was rumoured that mail was coming aboard. After so many people had promised to write to me I expected quite a bundle of post. A large mailbag was brought into the Fiddery and the contents spilled onto the floor and sorted out by a rush of eager hands. Names were called out as letters were found for friends. 'Hey Taffy, this one smells OK!' someone commented as he sniffed a purple-coloured envelope on which the address was written in a female hand. Taffy made a grab for the letter, fearing it would be kept from him for a joke. He hurriedly opened it and started reading whilst walking slowly to a seat away from everyone else. I waited with mounting anticipation for my letters. At last my name was called – my heart beat faster – it was a parcel – but then my heart sank. It was only my duvet jacket which I had asked my mother to forward to me. Much as I liked receiving letters from my family it was not the same as one from Sue. Her last words to me before I left were 'and I will write.' Being only two flights a week into Port Stanley perhaps her letters had been delayed, or maybe she had written to the address in Montevideo. She had a very busy life and perhaps she had not had time to write, but there again, perhaps she did not feel for me what I felt for her. I really didn't know. But what I did know all too painfully at that time was that whilst some of the other lads had half a dozen or more long letters, I did not receive any. I went to bed very depressed, although I tried not to show it, and went to sleep an uneasy man. Next morning we had the chance to see Port Stanley in the light of day. We could see the tiny 'cathedral', Stanley House (the Governor's residence), the main post office and the neat little rows of tidy looking painted houses on the hill side. I spent most of the morning writing more letters and masses of postcards. I was sorely tempted not to bother after the dearth of post the previous evening.

One of the benefits of an expedition on as large a scale as ours was that from amongst the men, considerable artistic talent was present. Three men were particularly adroit at folk music; King Fid Dougy, *Bransfield's* First Mate and General Assistant 'Foggy' starred in an *ad hoc* folk session at the 'Rose' pub. Foggy played his squeeze box and Dougy and First Mate played their fiddles. The atmosphere in there was excellent; the peat fire gave off a distinctive aroma which mixed with the pungent smells of a variety of tobaccos, and added to the odours of the ales. A good time was had by all. The next day was the Battle of the Falklands Day to commemorate the famous battle in the First World War. A communion service had been especially arranged for us. What surprised me was that there were nine or ten of us wanting to go, and Jerry was one of them. The service was conducted by a rather aged retired vicar who was visiting Port Stanley for a few weeks from Buenos Aires. Despite his years he raced through the service in no time, far too quickly for anyone to appreciate the fellowship, to meditate in the quiet, to pray in the peaceful calm, to absorb the Scriptures or to fully grapple with the challenges of the Gospels. But it was really good to have been able to have had that service. It bolstered me up for a considerable time to come.

After the service there was a military march past by the Royal Marines and the Falkland Islands Defence Force. The General Salute was taken by the Governor of the Falkland Islands who was resplendent in his smart uniform complete with gold braid, sword, and white pith helmet with its plume of ostrich feathers. It was a grand occasion with many of the islanders watching the neatly turned out soldiers, albeit so few of them as the entire garrison was no more than forty strong. The marching was accompanied by the traditional military music which was produced from a tape recorder and played over a loud speaker. After the salutes, the Governor proudly strutted to his limousine which was a purple London taxi on which a small Union Flag fluttered on the bonnet and the Emblem of the islands was painted smartly on the car doors. He was then driven the several hundred yards back to his residence. So ended the day's formal public celebrations and began the usual and customary celebrations with alcoholic beverages.

We had reached the part of our journey south where the travelling had become less routine and correspondingly more hazardous. We were about to leave the latitudes through which air and sea journeys are commonplace to climes which few men ever have the opportunity to experience at first hand. Everyone had returned to the ship from town. The crew busily prepared to weigh anchor and, as if suspecting the worst, checked that the hold covers were securely fastened. The ship's hooter blared out over the bleak and blustery harbour as the clank of the massive anchor chain rattled into its hold, accompanied by an increased thump-thump from the engines signalling our departure southwards. Most of us had taken the opportunity of the calm water of Stanley harbour to break out our kit bags and change into our warmer Antarctic-issue clothing. The red tartan woolly shirt itched with its newness and the grey moleskin trousers felt assuringly warm. I felt very self-conscious as I stepped out of my cabin in my pristine gear and headed for one of the decks to watch Stanley fade into the watery distance. A blast of cold air struck me as I emerged on deck into the bracing wind. I was glad I had heeded the advice of my more experienced colleagues and donned the warmer garb. Once we cleared the narrows and passed Pembroke Point the increasing strength of the wind became apparent. This was it. No turning back now. How long until we saw Stanley again I wondered, knowing full well that there was no guarantee of return. On one hand there was the excitement of venturing into new areas of experience, of challenge, of discovery. On the other, there was the fearful anticipation of a hostile unknown, a four-day voyage across the most notorious stretch of ocean in the world, let alone the hazards of the great icy continent that had eluded the great explorers for so long. The excitement won, pushing the negative thoughts into the background. I was enjoying this. However, my enjoyment was short-lived. As the ship turned southwards to skirt East Falkland so the sea became choppier, the white caps of the waves being whipped up by a 40 knot wind. The ship began to roll and pitch unevenly. Clouds of sea spray began to lash the foredecks. I had to stay on deck and watch; it was awe inspiring. The olivine-green sea stretched to the horizon; white horses punctuated the sea scape with their frothy streaks, still more did the ship pitch and yaw, roll and heave, as did my stomach not long after. The further south we went the larger the waves seemed. The ship was now climbing up one side of a wave only to come thundering down into the trough, the bow plunging into the oncoming wave and taking a frighteningly long time to re-emerge. I had never seen such enormous waves. When we were in a trough the surrounding crests towered over the ship. The next moment we could see for miles as the ship was borne up by a crest only to disappear again, as it was released to crash back into the turbulent waters. Like many of my companions, I retired to my bunk, my face reflecting a similar hue to that of the stormy sea outside. As I lay there so I and my mattress slid in unison up and down the veneered bunk in response to the perpetual corkscrewing motion that *Bransfield* made as she valiantly battled her way painfully slowly southwards. The sounds of the storm outside were no comfort. Feeling like I had never felt before but how I was to feel on many future occasions, I prayed that the retching of my stomach would ease and that the storm would abate. Instead it went on hour after horrible hour.

Later during the afternoon we passed through the worst of the weather and life began to improve. By dinner time I felt well enough to risk a journey to the scradge palace for dinner. By the time I retired for the night, we had sailed only about one hundred miles. This was going to be a long journey.

Next morning, I was surprised at how well I felt and managed to do justice to each meal of the day. My time was spent reading and preparing my field kit, sewing up the seams on my jeans which were two inches too long in the leg. The end result was not exactly Savile Row but at least it served its purpose.

During the afternoon, we crossed another milestone, the Antarctic Convergence over which the air and sea temperatures fell by 4°C. We could no longer smell the sea and there were few, if any, birds following the ship. We were on our own.

With the calm in the weather and the general absence of anything definite with which to occupy my time, my thoughts meandered to the people I had left behind in England, especially Sue. I began to wonder about our relationship, what

I meant to her and what she meant to me, and how she was faring. It would be a long time before I was to see her again or had a letter from her, so all I could do was wonder. My lazy daydreaming was interrupted by a loud shout from the scradge palace. Food called and to add to the meal one of my fellow Fidlets was celebrating his birthday. After dinner, the revellers rolled and swayed their way into the Fiddery, their gait being influenced more by the wine than by the state of the sea.

Overnight the weather worsened and visibility decreased. Along with this came a growing sensation of excitement caused by the anticipation of approaching the last continent, the one that had been so elusive for so many years. The pictures of Antarctica that I had seen previously flashed across my mind's eye but with the ever present question 'Will it really be like this?' It was almost like waiting for a dental appointment in that the inevitable was going to happen and that one had no real control over it. Excitement was tempered by tiredness and once the day's log book had been written up and I had had my quiet time I was ready for sleep, even though as near midnight as it was, it was still daylight outside.

Next day started off in a somewhat more subdued fashion than the day before, it only because a fair number of people on board had hefty hangovers. Being a Sunday, it was Captain's Inspection, 10.30 hours sharp; so those who could tidied up their cabins and swabbed down the corridors and public rooms. The swish-swash of a mop slopped along a shiny floor; a resounding crash of a dropped metal bucket was greeted with multi-coloured language from a hungover Fid. For the duration of the inspection we had to be out of our cabins so I equipped myself with my camera gear in order to photograph Cape Pigeons whose numbers were increasing as we approached land. After nearly an hour on the helicopter deck I had taken only four shots. The birds just would not oblige when I was ready or, if they did, I fumbled the camera in the chill of the wind. After dinner, a few of us were up on deck enjoying the fresh air, peering over the ship's handrail into the distance, just watching. The sea had calmed down considerably and a sea mist had developed which reduced visibility to around half a mile or so. Suddenly, someone noticed a huge shadow in the mist off our port side. Silently, a vast blue-green form loomed from the shrouding mist, its bulk passive yet menacing, slow yet apparently unstoppable. It was my first glimpse of an iceberg and it was a very eerie experience. No one spoke, all just stared overwhelmed by the icy leviathan. The proverbial tip of the iceberg was as large as our ship. The realisation that 90% of that *Marie Celeste* was there but hidden beneath the cold black sea and seemingly so close was awe inspiring. The ice was a most beautiful azure blue with a brilliant white icing on top. Waves had sculpted fantastic shapes in the ice and had smoothed a platform on which a cluster of penguins sheltered from the elements. Surf breaking over the lowest edges of the berg revealed a seal prowling in the water. As suddenly as it had appeared the berg merged again into the blanketing mist. What we had witnessed was a performance of an act which had been staged millions of times but had played to few audiences before. Not long after, a second iceberg appeared, this time with no passengers but an equal in its magnificent art form to the one that had passed by previously. The berg with its arches and deep blue caves incised beneath its flat top was silhouetted against a grey-white horizon beneath a purple blanket of thick cloud. This berg too drifted quietly on its way north to the graveyard of icebergs, the warmer waters of the lower latitudes. But for the need of sleep I could have watched the icebergs all night.

When I woke up next morning I realised that the steady throb of the ship's engines had ceased and the ship was stationary. I jumped out of my bunk and rushed to the porthole. When I drew aside the curtain I was greeted by brilliant sunshine in a cloudless sky over one of the most incredible views I had ever seen. During the night we had anchored off Hope Bay at the northern tip of the Antarctic Peninsula, and my cabin being on the landward side of the ship, I was treated to an amazingly beautiful scene. Sharp peaked mountains, three thousand or more feet high stood majestically around the bay with blue-white stoles of ice around their shoulders. Their ice fronts formed impressive ice cliffs from which blocks of ice fell occasionally into the blue sea and mingled with the many small icebergs which littered the bay. Some seals lazed basking in the sun's warmth on brilliant white ice floes. Penguins porpoised through the water at unbelievable speeds and with remarkable ease, in such contrast to their land-based antics where they waddled like starchy butlers in evening dress. So this was Antarctica! Near the foreshore, just up from the beach stood a small hut, black against the sparkling snow around it. This was the British refuge from which two geologists and their mountaineer assistants were to work for part of the summer. Separated from the tiny building, some half a mile or so to the south were the brightly painted red huts which formed the Argentinian base 'Esperanza'. The human population consisted of militia and several families with six children in all and eleven more people due to arrive within a fortnight. Apparently the intention of the Argentinians was to build a school, a small church and adequate living accommodation for the township. All this was part of the Argentine strategy to claim the Antarctic Peninsula as their territory. Much to the consternation of the senior staff who landed to inspect the British hut, they were welcomed by an Argentinian Harbour Master and an Immigration Officer who tried to insist on marking passports with an entry stamp to the Antarctic portion of the Argentinian Republic, despite the fact that this was contrary to the prevailing Antarctic Treaty. Our British contingent did not comply but the situation became politically rather sensitive, especially as it was related to the problems over the Falkland Islands. The incident was not isolated, as a further visit to an Argentinian base later in the season was similarly awkward, at least to begin with. Whilst the goings-on continued on shore, those of us left on board lined the guard rails on deck and watched the panorama before us. For those of us new to Antarctica, our introduction to the continent was truly unforgettable. The whole place was alive. The water was teeming with activity with the penguins and the seals; dozens of birds hovered around the ship gleaning scraps of food thrown by Fids or hopped annoyingly around a basking seal picking up the fishy remains from an unfinished meal. The ice floes bobbed up and down with the waves making sloshing and gurgling sounds as the jumble of floating ice jostled together. This was far better than anything I had expected and provided a foretaste of what was to come. The cry of the seagulls seemed out of place somehow as I associated the sound with my home in Falmouth; a familiar haunting cry in a place which felt so different to anything I had experienced before. I was itching to go ashore but it was not for me on this occasion. Mingled with this feeling was one of wanting to share the emotional reaction to such overwhelming beauty with someone close. I thought of Sue and I felt alone. The ship's siren sounded and broke my thoughts. The shore party returned soon after, and before long we were under way sailing further south amidst a darkening sky and a freshening breeze.

3: To First Base

As *Bransfield* sailed steadily southwards so the weather improved. The clouds gradually lifted to reveal superb sharp peaks dwarfing the enormous glaciers, and sheer ice cliffs teetering on the water's edge. The ship cut through the calm, almost mirror-like water, sending smooth ripples astern to distort the reflections of the magnificent scenery. The ship's rails were leant upon by rows of Fidlets speechless at the spectacular vision before them. One, a builder destined for Rothera, turned to me and said, sighing, 'This is just too much to take in all at one go. I've had enough,' and he went below. The rumble of the ship's engines was the only noise to be heard in an otherwise silent world. We knew that we were being treated to the best of the weather and the least inhospitable conditions that Antarctica could afford. What struck me was that despite the calm and the silence there was an awesome power. I could not really describe it or identify it specifically, but it was there and it could be felt. Perhaps it was the knowledge that behind the icy facade which we could see so resplendent before us, was an immense force which has been in action for millions of years and over which man had no control. The ice was flowing down to the sea, there either to melt into oblivion or to break off into icebergs or smaller ice fragments to drift north and thence to disappear. Rocks which poked through the cold white blanket as nunataks* had been shattered by the tremendous cold or ground into powder by the seemingly static ice above or even grooved by rocks caught at the base of the ice and used like chisels to carve the characteristic signature of glaciation. In the foreground nearer the ship, seals lay basking in the sun, letting the world pass them by as they dozed their lives away. Penguins swam through the water in chaotic groups, or stood preening themselves in ranks upon ice floes which bobbed gently in the swell. As the ship reached further into southerly latitudes so the ice floes became larger and more plentiful. In places, the sea ice formed large expanses of flat featureless white over which penguins waddled, leaving sinuous trails. The ship pushed aside the smaller floes with her specially shaped bow. Sometimes a larger floe would be submerged completely under the bow only to bob up with a swoosh of frothing water some moments later along the ship's side. When I first saw this happen I was surprised to see that the underside of the ice floes was not white like I had expected but was red or brown. At first I thought that this was paint which had been rubbed off the ship's hull by the passage of the rough coarse-grained ice. I later found out that this discolouration was due to the presence of tiny organisms called diatoms which exist in plentitude in these waters. Once, an unsuspecting penguin was tipped off its floe by the ship ploughing her way south. The ice floes were deceptively massive with many being of similar weight to *Bransfield*. When the ship hit them she shuddered on impact and slowed almost to a stop before pushing aside the icy obstacle. In other cases ice floes would crack and the ship then passed through between the fragments which jostled in the water like ice cubes in a giant cocktail. Passing one massive ice cliff we watched a large ice tower collapse into the green water below; it all happened as if it was in slow motion with the sound reaching our ears after the action had happened. There was no chance of being bored. The whole place was alive. Our first stopping point was Palmer Station, an American base on Anvers Island. Tied alongside the base's jetty was MV *Hero*, a trawler used by the Americans as a support vessel for their work in this area. We had been told *Hero* was small but she was more like a motorised scow. We were all warmly greeted, partly through cupboard love because we had their year's supply of food on board. Our first evening there was truly memorable. The sun hung low on the horizon and cast a beautiful glow to the dusk sky, with oranges and pinks in the clouds reflected in the glassy black water of the bay. As the sun altered its position so the whole mood of the scene changed; in early evening there was a warm pink tinge which gradually faded to a cold blue glow. The gentle sunlight picked out the subtle colours in the ice cliff nearby, with faint hues of pinks and greens within the bluey white of the cliff face. Above the towering ice, the full moon cast its glow, the dark maria clearly visible. I spent several hours on the *Bransfield's* top deck enjoying the heat of the sun before it sank too low. The heat was relative for the air temperature was only 2°C, but the glow of the sun's rays was warming in the breezeless air.

The next day was similarly fine so I was able to spend the morning taking photographs and shooting cine film. During this time one of the BAS Twin Otter aircraft flew in from Rothera Station with a Fid on board who had had an accident involving battery acid and required medical attention from one of the several doctors on board *Bransfield*. Just before landing the plane flew past one of the ice cliffs whilst banking and the noise of the engines triggered off a large and spectacular fall of ice blocks which cascaded into the water below.

After an uninspired lunch on board ship, I was assigned to a work party to shift cargo in Hold Number 2. We were involved in manhandling around 36,000 items of alcoholic drink for the base. It was also quite revealing to see what kind of food our American colleagues were being treated to courtesy of the National Science Foundation: frozen lobster, prime T-bone steaks and so on and so forth. Handling all that food made me really hungry by dinner time.

Next day Jerry and I walked up to the airstrip on the ice sheet near the base. Once at the top the view was breathtaking and the quiet truly incredible. We could hear penguins and seals which were at least a mile away from us in the bay. Noise from the ship carried easily too. Once over the brow of the hill and out of sight of the base all previous sounds vanished into an eerie silence. The sun was sufficiently strong for us to walk around shirtless. I soon had to replace my shirt, not from the cold surprisingly but to avoid being burnt by the sun, a common problem in Antarctica in summer. We returned to Palmer Station and had a good look around inside. It was very comfortable and had very modern amenities. One aspect of the station which set it apart from its British equivalent was that the Base personnel included three women. Two of them were senior members of the base whereas the third woman was considerably younger and more attractive. I thought that could have led to quite a few social problems on the station, especially after the drink had been flowing. Having a mixed staff could have generated a lot of sexual tension as well as in-fighting amongst the men to curry favours with the one eligible lady.

One feature of work parties was that they provided an opportunity to meet and become better acquainted with my fellow Fids. One man, a driver, thought himself a paragon of virtue and was surprised when some of his colleagues did not concur with his opinion. Another man seemed to have distinct difficulty with the English language for his conversation consisted of four letter expletives linked by the occasional word of acceptable language. Both men I found overpowering and I tried to keep out of their way as much as circumstances would allow. Avoidance, in this case, was the first secret of tolerance. Most of the other Fids I found most amenable and friendly and the considerable variety of social, educational and professional experience made meeting them pleasant and rewarding. I learned a lot, not only about other walks of life but about life itself.

After two and a half days at Palmer Station, we set sail for Faraday Base on the Argentine Islands. The weather improved into yet another glorious day. The mists and haze lifted bit by bit gradually yielding to view the magnificent rocky peaks, black in contrast to the brilliant white of the ice. The water was as calm as a mill pond as we entered the Lemaire Channel, where contorted and disintegrating glaciers descended near vertical slopes as if clinging to the rock for survival. Small irregular icebergs and growlers* testified that gravity had claimed some ice. We came across black ice – ice laden with dirt or so clean it was transparent and all that could be seen was like floating clear glass with the black colour of the sea seen through it. Towards the southern end of the channel we encountered yet more pack ice. This gave way to clear water for a while, but nearing the Argentine Islands we entered fast ice*. Here our progress was severely hampered. *Bransfield* could only go so far before stopping because the thickness of the sea ice was too great for her to break her way through. The ship went full astern for several hundred yards then full ahead straight at the ice. On impact the whole ship jarried. On deck I had to hold on or risk being toppled over with a jolt. The ship rose up on to the ice for half its length. Luckily the weight of the ship was sufficient to fragment the ice barrier which popped up on both sides of the ship amidst frothing water, grinding growlers and brash*. We made painfully slow progress. During the afternoon Faraday Base came into view although still over a mile distant. During the whole of this delay I was up on deck enjoying the sunshine and the view. The Argentine Islands consisted of a series of fairly flat-lying rocky islands some ten or so miles off the west coast of the Antarctic Peninsula which provides a spectacular if not lethal backdrop of Alpine-looking mountains. Some of these peaks were over 5,000 feet high. Sadly they had claimed the lives of three of my colleagues a couple of years previously; they disappeared during a storm and their bodies were never found despite extensive air and ground searches.

Amongst the miriad profusion of ice floes, penguins and seals could be seen in plenty. Skuas chanced an untimely end by landing too close to apparently immobile but deceptively fast moving seals. Wilson Stormy Petrels danced like fairies dipping their feet ever so delicately onto the water leaving barely a ripple in their search for food. The wildlife provided unending pleasure and entertainment with its antics, especially those of the ever-comic penguins. Surely God must have a sense of humour to have thought of such amusing birds.

After dinner we Fids were treated to our film show which we had every three days. During the screening of the film, *Bransfield* was still trying to force her way through fast-ice by the ahead/astern routine. Each time she hit the ice again, everyone watching the film jolted and groaned as some people who were unprepared or unbalanced at the time of impact fell off their seats and upset drinks.

At the end of the cinema session we discovered that we had come to a standstill and were icebound. We were allowed off the ship onto the sea ice. The top few inches consisted of soft snow but underneath was the tough concrete-like sea ice. We kept clear of obvious danger zones close to icebergs and near cracks which were easy to spot. But there was a vast area of undisturbed safe ice on which to vent out frustrations. We played football which was hard work in the soft snow, but it provided an important release of energy after sitting cooped up in the ship for several days, and was great fun. We also had an indigenous spectator – a penguin had waddled up to see what was going on. It stood by the edge of what was roughly our pitch and watched, occasionally turning its head to preen itself, obviously bored with the action. It received quite a surprise, however, when it suddenly came face to face with a badly mis-kicked black and white football. The penguin looked at the ball which had stopped only a couple of feet away from it then turned and fled, perhaps mistaking the ball for a rather obese penguin. We eventually retired to bed somewhat tired but happy around midnight.

Next morning *Bransfield* restarted her attempts at breaking through the ice towards Faraday. By 2 pm we were icebound again. This time it was for fear of forcing a route between two menacing icebergs which, had we cracked the ice surrounding them, might have been blown by the wind and trapped us restricting any moves to extricate ourselves from the sea ice which had claimed rather too many ships before us.

During the remainder of the afternoon, I wrote to Sue telling her of all my adventures since my last epistle to her. I do not think I had ever enjoyed letter writing so much as then. It really seemed to make the miles disappear. It was very pleasant to reminisce about our times together in Bromley, to guess what she might have been involved in with the church, and what she might have been thinking about me. But these thoughts were dangerous as they led to total unsupported speculation. Such thoughts often prayed on Fids during their time south, frequently with dire consequences upon their return home. Also during the afternoon I had the good opportunity to spend time learning about plant fossils from Tim Jefferson, a research geologist who was carrying out field work towards his doctorate in conjunction with BAS. But being icebound made be feel restless. Would I ever get into the field to start my research?

The following day, *Bransfield* continued battling her way through the ice towards Faraday. At 2.10 pm the ship's hooter blared and an orange flare was fired off to signal that we had arrived at Faraday. Fids on deck cheered and morale took a noticeable upturn. Within the hour *Bransfield* had dropped anchor and the re-supply of the base had started and was to last for the next five days. I was involved in man-handling 40 kg sacks of building aggregate on the first day. Two Fids would lift each sack onto a third Fid's shoulder and he would then carry the sack up the beach from the scow to where the new buildings were to be sited, dump the sack on an ever increasing pile, then return to the scow for the next sack. Each man shifted about 2 tonnes that day, and 50 tonnes of aggregate were landed. This was hot work and most of us were in shirtsleeves despite the fact that it was snowing for much of the time. The main trouble was that some sacks had holes in them and as they were being carried laboriously up the beach, a trickle of sand went down one's neck. By the end of the day we were caked in grime. Temporary respite came at smokoh* time when we were able to seek sanctuary inside the old base. A large pot of tea had been brewed; it tasted like the elixir of life. The hard work gave us all healthy appetites. It also gave us considerable muscle and backaches and our shoulders seemed to droop more than before our arrival at Faraday. At the end of the day, those of us not scheduled to stay at Faraday over the summer returned to the ship for the night, leaving our colleagues on the base to settle in.

The next day we had to shift steel mesh, large melt-water tanks and very heavy steel plates for a new Braithewait fuel tank. We also had to move more construction materials, glass, concrete and aggregate, wood and general materials. The final unloading job was to disembark three rather large electric generators. These had to be winched up the beach on wooden plattens as they were far too heavy to even contemplate lifting. As a treat, the Base cook gave us something special at smokoh. He produced bacon sandwiches and pancakes with maple syrup as well as the requisite tea and biscuits. At one point during the unloading of the aggregate from the scow, an inquisitive Gentou penguin came ashore and stood watching the proceedings from a safe distance. Soon it was back in the water and we thought it had swum away. Next thing we knew was a swoosh of water and our wet feathered friend was standing on a sack in the bottom of the scow, having made a perfect leap from the water, over the side and into the bottom. The poor bird looked rather surprised and lost as from where it was standing it could no longer see the water. It wandered around in the scow squawking in bewilderment. It managed to hop up to the top edge of the scow from where it could see the water. However, it could not work out how to position itself to dive back into the water. While it was still pondering its plight, a Faraday Fid grabbed the bird and threw it into the sea. Never had I seen a penguin look so surprised as that one did just before hitting the water feet first, a most unorthodox mode of entry for a penguin.

When ashore and not involved in a work party I managed to have a look around the island as far as it was safe to do. These islands had played an important role in the historic exploration of the Antarctic Peninsula as it was in a cove just around from the base that SS *Penola* overwintered during the British Graham Land Expedition 1934–37. Now these islands were host to the permanent British research base, the materials for whose expansion we had just landed. When the weather was fine enough, the scenery was most photogenic, especially in an evening light. Eventually all our work was completed at Faraday and it was time to set sail again, this time northwards to Damoy, a summer air facility used by BAS to ferry men and limited supplies to destinations further south which were barred to ships by ice or geographical position. We sailed back through the Lemaire Channel with no problems at all; the sea ice which had caused the earlier delays had been blown out to sea during the recent inclement weather. During the voyage north, I found my thoughts turning more to my imminent disembarkation than to the beauty of the scenery. At last my chance was drawing nearer to go ashore and fly to my research area to begin my work. I became increasingly nervous at the thought. The ship had become my home and gave me security, warmth and a social life. To go ashore was a real step into circumstances likely to test me beyond anything that I had encountered before. It was a great challenge and, though nervous, I was prepared to accept it. As we neared out next destination I busied myself in readiness for the following stage of my journey.

By mid-afternoon we had arrived at Damoy. From the ship I could see two small buildings, the larger of which was to be our base for the next day or so until we could be picked up and flown south by air. The second building was a tiny shed which purported to be a refuge and was owned by the Argentines. Our hut nestled on the flanks of an ice promontory several hundred feet high. Its flattish top provided a rudimentary but adequate skiway for the short landing/short take-off Twotters*. Snow covered everywhere bar a few rocky outcrops claimed by a penguin rookery. Across the bay were the mountains on the eastern side of Anvers Island, and these sharp peaks provided a textured icy canvas for the evening colours. Soon after dropping anchor we went ashore with the first batch of personal gear. We returned to the ship for what was to be, all being well, our last night on board until the end of the season.

The launch hung from the davits, wobbling as we climbed aboard. As the launch chugged away from the ship our colleagues on deck waved us cheerio. The trip from the ship to shore did not take long; as we headed off towards Damoy the Brantub faded into the whiteness of a blizzard. We stood on shore and watched the launch return to her mother ship. In a matter of minutes, *Bransfield* was under way. With a parting couple of blasts on the hooter she slipped away northwards out of sight. The wind slapped around us with large flakes of soft snow, and howled through the guys holding down the roof of the hut. We were alone; ashore at last, with only the sounds of the elements and the penguins to keep us company. Our only contact now with the outside world was via the radio in the hut. If any of us had forgotten anything, it was too bad. If one of us had had an accident it would have taken a considerable amount of time for the ship to return to give assistance. Our only way out of Damoy was by aircraft. However, with poor weather, this was not to happen until after Christmas. So we had to prepare ourselves for our own special Christmas at Damoy, one of the whitest Christmasses on earth.

4: Christmas

The Damoy hut was soon ship-shape with our equipment installed. With nine of us indoors, the single living room was easily crowded. Before very long a roaring primus stove gave us a fresh brew of tea which was readily imbibed. There was not much to do but wait until the weather improved before we stood any chance of an aircraft paying us a visit. Thus it was necessary to busy ourselves as much as possible to help pass the time. Although the weather was poor with fresh snow falling and a stiff breeze, a colleague and I went to visit the penguin colony down by the water's edge. The gentou penguins were lying on their stomachs with their backs to the wind. Beneath them were their eggs, commonly two in number, being kept warm by the bird's body heat. This protection also served to keep the eggs from their main predator, the skua, of which there were several at the edge of the rookery just waiting their chance for a dash at an unguarded nest to pinch the egg and eat its contents.

As it was Christmas Eve, we strung Christmas cards around the room on pieces of twine. We raided the paperback library and then retired to a quiet corner to while away the time. Our first meal in the hut was a mixture of field rations and goodies* given to us by the cook on board *Bransfield*. After the meal most of us went outside and snowballed each other for a while until someone had the idea of using the skidoos* as well. Two people fired up the 'doos and started racing round the hut. The remainder of us then started to throw snowballs at the two riders in attempts at knocking them off their vehicles, which was quite hair-raising at times as these 'doos could achieve up to about 40 miles an hour. We then graduated to sledging down the flank of the ice airstrip towards the hut. A skidoo towed the heavy sledge up the slope then up to four people would risk all in a frantic descent. Often people fell off en route to the bottom, only to hitch a ride on the next 'doo to the top to repeat their escapade. On one descent, I was in charge of steering and two others sat behind. Things soon got out of control with the sledge snaking its way with increasing speed towards the Argentine refugio. My two companions dived off into the soft snow to avoid what they thought would be the inevitable, but I stayed on until the end, just managing to bring the sledge to a standstill only a few feet from the tiny hut. We fell about with laughter almost to the point of being incapacitated. It was great fun; I have never enjoyed 'winter' sports so much as then. Some two and a half hours of physical sport rendered us exhausted and ready for a quieter evening in the hut. The general bonhomie engendered by the outside sports set the scene for a very pleasant Christmas Eve. As the sunset developed outside, so the Tilley Lamps created their own glow with their characteristic gentle hiss, making a special comfortable atmosphere inside. We supped hot toddies of whisky, and Tia Maria, to see in Christmas Day and to drink the health of absent friends, family and muffins*.

Breakfast on Christmas morning was a very tardy affair, ending nearer the afternoon than the usual breakfast time. This did not concern us unduly as time was purely academic there – we had no schedule to which to keep, no formalities, just nine men in an isolated hut with time on our hands. If we managed to stave off boredom then that was fine by us. We started on the preparations for our special dinner in the early afternoon. One feature of the hut was a hut log-book in which, for every day the hut was occupied, an entry was to be made. As it was Christmas we decided to leave as that day's entry an illuminated dinner menu which Dave Brittain, an ex-graphic designer, concocted for us. We started eating around 3.30 pm and the meal lasted for over four hours, although the later courses were still being consumed intermittently until well into the evening. The meal was really quite delightful, a supreme example of Fid ingenuity and improvisation. What drink there was flowed freely, laughter was in great abundance and a good time was had by all. We played silly games like charades, guessing the names of famous people, and so on. Eventually we tired of thinking so much and ended up with yet more coffee and eats. Despite the hilarity of the day, all of us contemplated for at least a short time our own Christmas within the framework of the communal festivities which we had enjoyed. The toasts to absent friends, family and girlfriends caused a mixed response. To some it was good riddance; they were glad to be out of it all. For others, including myself, there was some disappointment at not being able to share the fun and festivities with people I loved. I imagined all the parties taking place in Bromley over the Christmas holidays, Sue and all my other good friends enjoying themselves and I wondered if they would be drinking my health at all. And then there were the church services that I was missing where the real meaning and purpose of Christmas, the birth of Christ, was being celebrated. How far removed could we have been from the first Christmas those 1982 years or so before in Bethlehem! We were in a tiny hut cut off from the outside world on the most remove continent on the globe. All we had for company apart from ourselves were the penguins and seals. But then, I thought, despite the fact that we had snow outside, we were near a desert, albeit a cold one. There was no hotel and it was cramped and at times uncomfortable. It made me think that perhaps in Antarctica we had more in common physically with that first Christmas than most people in the civilised world. We did not have the distraction of the same old television films, the trite greetings, the plastic decorations or superficial cards which all too frequently made no mention of the significance of the occasion or why we should be celebrating it, just a cold looking robin with a stupid scarf around its neck next to a crimson bauble, or an eighteenth century coach and horses. We were also saved the tension of buying presents for people, many of whom we would rather not have to spend out on. Nor were we subjected to the ridiculous pre-Christmas build up which seemed to start earlier each year, nor to all the blatant commercialism. The usual Christmas had always felt to me like an over-inflated balloon. On Boxing Day it deflates a bit, then pops up after New Year's Day leaving one with a soggy limp anti-climax to take one into the new year. This Antarctic Christmas made me realise just how much of a masquerade Christmas had become for me back home. I was glad of the reminder of Christ's birthday, as it focused my attention on not only his birth but the reasons for his arrival, his life and ministry and his death and resurrection. Instead of that dreary start to the year I had promise of a good year ahead and Easter to look forward to.

* * *

On Boxing Day morning, a colleague and I went to the penguin rookery to carry out a census. We had to count the number of birds on nests, their number of eggs (which were as large as goose eggs) and the number of isolated individuals. All this was easier said than done. The rookery was spread over thirty-three rock outcrops. As we moved from one to the next, so several lone penguins preceded us so we had to be very careful not to include them. Some penguins would not oblige and let us look to see how many eggs they had and so we had to nudge them out of the way. The eager parents guarded their offspring bravely, squawking furiously and making pecking motions. Fortunately, their beaks missed our hands otherwise they could have inflicted nasty wounds. We counted 875 nests with 1080 individuals present in the rookery at the time. These numbers indicated that the total rookery population was more in the region of 1750–2000 birds; many of the brooding parents were at sea feeding in preparation for their turn sitting on the nest for several weeks to enable the other parent to go to sea to feed in its turn.

Part of our time at the hut was spent carrying out chores which we each took in turns. Water was obtained by shovelling fresh snow into a water barrel which comprised two parts; the upper portion contained the snow and the lower part was a paraffin stove. The meagre facilities at the hut included an outside toilet, i.e., a walk to the beach to the water's edge. In a full snow storm and gale force freezing cold winds, bodily functions became quite epic affairs and brevity was encouraged!

I noticed that the general standard of language had fallen, with expletives and blasphemies becoming more abundant. I found that I was not immune and so I had to pay considerable attention to what I said. I hoped to be a good Christian witness by my actions and by what I left unsaid as well as what I did say. I was finding it difficult to have quiet times for reading my Bible and praying if only because of the light in the bunk room. I endeavoured to start earlier, before the shutters went up. The trouble with twenty-four hours of daylight was trying to shut the light out at night. It was too dim to read comfortably but sufficiently light to be distracting when trying to go to sleep.

Our early morning radio schedule with Rothera the following day did not sound too hopeful regarding an airlift but we packed our gear so that should we be given only a moment's notice we would be prepared. To pass the time I strolled down to the bay to see what I could find of interest. There were boulders of rock types indicative of the violent geological history of the area – lavas and breccias*, and metamorphic* rocks. I found a stranded krill, a shrimp-like creature orange in colour with two parallel white stripes along its back. I took this specimen back to the hut in the hope of keeping it. Proper biological preservatives were not available so I used Grappa Blanca, an Argentinian white wine more suited to pickling than drinking.

In the early afternoon at the next radio sched* we were told that a plane was on its way, so at 6 pm we were ready with all the gear at the airstrip on top of the ice promontory. A few minutes later the plane was spotted, a tiny pinprick against the great mountains behind. The Twotter circled four times inspecting the airstrip and testing for side-winds before dropping and landing. It taxied right up to us then turned to face back down the skiway in readiness for take-off. With so many pairs of eager hands, loading the gear did not take long and we were soon ready for departure. We all had to squeeze into the tail end of the plane to help with the liftoff. One of the problems with ski-planes was that the nose ski might have stuck to the snow and so hindered take-off. The weight of the passengers aft of the mid-fuselage skis offset the snow adhesion and helped the plane to lift off safely. Once airborne, the passengers could then redistribute themselves more comfortably for the flight. Our pilot pushed the throttles forward with his right hand and gripped the joy stick firmly as the plane accelerated along the rough ski-way. He tried hard to keep the plane speeding straight and to avoid slipping down either side of the considerably cambered runway. The drone of the engines was deafening, but very quickly the plane reached full speed and shot off the end of the ice promontory over the edge of a large ice cliff and became airborne. We climbed quickly, banked and headed south. Trying to ignore the nauseous feelings in my stomach I was pleased and relieved at being on my way at last. We flew at very low level through the Lemaire Channel, banking steeply past irregularly sculpted icebergs, flashing past the flanking rock strata which were once part of a volcano whose vent had long since disappeared. In just 15 minutes we were over Faraday rolling the wings like a victory salute at only a few hundred feet altitude. We then climbed to 10,000 feet. The views from that altitude were out of this world. Being above any clouds we could see for many tens of miles in every direction, and were able to see the whole length of some glaciers, from the height of the Palmer Land plateau winding down through the coastal mountain ranges to the sea where the glaciers broke up into icebergs and growlers and bergy bits, and where the continental ice of considerable age, possibly many tens of thousands of years old, met the sea ice only one winter or two in age. The sea ice was punctuated by icebergs trapped in its frozen grasp, only to be released during the summer warmth or by the ferocity of a storm breaking up the sea ice and blowing it out to sea. It was quite an experience to contrast the modes of transport I had been on in the past week. From a ship which took several days to travel from Damoy to Faraday to a speedy plane which covered the same distance in just quarter of an hour. Not only that, I could appreciate the benefit that aircraft had made in the major advances in our knowledge of the geography of the Antarctic Peninsula. Before the 1930s very little was known other than what was observed from ships which, like *Bransfield* and her sister ship RRS *John Biscoe*, braved the ice to venture into southern waters in the furtherance of man's knowledge of his planet. In the late 1930s a seaplane had been used to route spot for land parties for the British Graham Land Expedition. The photographs taken during these flights with the pilot's own observations led to major advances in the maps of the area. Without these aircraft BAS could not have hoped to have achieved even a fraction of what had been. Our flight to Rothera lasted but one and a half hours and after circling we landed safely and smoothly at the skiway some three miles west of the base. Some Fids from the base manned the flight caboose for radio communications with both the aircraft and the base while others stood by with the fire fighting sledge just in case anything untoward should happen. Several more were ready to offload equipment and to ferry the new arrivals off the ice piedmont and down to the base in a snow-cat*, a caterpillared tractor. At the main door of the principal building, Dave Fletcher, the Base Commander met us. He showed us around and briefly explained the safety aspects of the place and the important rooms and facilities. I was amazed at the base. It was very modern and extremely comfortable. Accommodation was on the ground floor in bunk rooms mostly with four berths to each. There was a well stocked library with a wide variety of books. It was tradition that everyone who stayed at a BAS base should bring with them as many books as they could and donate them to the base library. The wash rooms had chemical toilets and smart showers although water was a problem. In winter the men had to cut snow blocks for the water tanks, as at Damoy and in summer there was to be a desalination plant taking salt water from the bay to the south of the base. Upstairs was the main scradge palace, a very well equipped kitchen, a bar and lounge area which had been designed and constructed by the over-wintering Fids the year before. The bar wall was bedecked with plaques from visiting ships of many nationalities. There was a hi-fi unit with a wide selection of records and tapes and a rolled-up screen for those frequent but dreadful films. That evening I met Peter who was to be my General Assistant (GA) for the summer. He had had one year on base already and was well experienced with plenty of high-quality mountaineering behind him. Over the winter he had checked through and repaired the field equipment designated for our use over the coming months, and I tried to give him some reasonable rationale for some of my scientific plans. It was strange to begin with on base, in new surroundings with a different way of doing things compared with either the ship or Faraday. The strangest thing of all was joining a community which had become tightly knit over the winter months. We summer-only personnel were like intruders ill at ease on someone else's patch. In conversation, there would be many in-jokes to which we would not be party and communal experiences of winter events that we could not share. On their part some expressed envy that we, by living in Cambridge during the Austral winter, had had a social life so that we had experiences which they could not share. This barrier faded in time as we all had our jobs to do and had to do them together. By then we all had one common objective, to make the summer season as successful as possible. Success was rated in terms of achievement of the goals for the field season. If work was left undone or major tasks were unfinished it was construed as only partial success. The reasons for the curtailment of work were normally due to bad weather. Occasionally, people made mistakes like forgetting an important piece of kit but in most cases Fid ingenuity found a way round such human error.

The day after our arrival we were shown around the rest of the base so that we would be familiar with the area in the case of an emergency. The greatest fear for that base was not running out of food, fuel or water, but the hazard of fire. The buildings were made of wood and were tinder dry. If a serious blaze had occurred the buildings would have gone up in flames very quickly. The destruction of the accommodation block in summer, let alone in mid-winter, would have been devastating, so we were all versed in fire fighting and evacuation drills. Every night of the year, one man was always on fire-watch, patrolling the base to keep a wary eye on safety.

My GA Peter took me to a small ice cliff near the base to remind me of certain basic field safety techniques. He showed me how to position Deadmen* and use a jockey winch in case of crevasse evacuations; he reminded me of how to use jumars* for ascending ropes. He also introduced me to several huskies, each as different from each other as chalk and cheese. Jimbo was a sad-looking seven-year-old who was suffering from a serious eye disease. He was soon to be shot, which was the kindest thing for him. Then there was a lively dog called Jacky who was an eighteen-month-old bitch. She was fluffy yet lion-like, ruffled yet tough, and her eyes had a steel hard look. However, she was as dopey as a dog could become and nestled down to allow me to tickle her tummy. Then there was a young puppy of about 8 months who looked very sorry for herself as she was rather ill. She was short haired, which is uncommon for Huskies. The last two I met, Thumper and Bambi, were also puppies. I climbed into their pen and was instantly overwhelmed by them as they leapt all over me in attempts to lick my face, bite my beard and undo my boot laces. The pups had been penned as they were still too young to be put with the rest of the huskies on the dog spans outside.

During the day, while Peter and I had been packing our kit into sledging boxes to fit on our sledges, the planes flew out a couple of field parties to begin their work. I could not help but feel envious. After all the delays so far I was still on base, and feeling increasingly frustrated.

After dinner I sat in the lounge and listened to Vivaldi's *Four Seasons*. I thought of Sue and of how we used to enjoy classical music together, she as the expert and me as the interested novice. The record soon put me in a melancholic mood, feelings of nostalgia mixed with doubts about our relationship. If only I could have spoken to her then. The best I could hope for was a letter and when would that arrive? I went out for a walk in the evening twilight and strolled towards the ice ramp to gain a better view over the base and the bay with the mountains of the main peninsula prominent across the water. The low sun cast a pink glow over the glaciers and the blue sky was reflected in the glassy black water. The blueness looked as cold as I felt in the chill of the breeze. If Sue were with me then, she would have appreciated not only the view but the experience of just being there. The Antarctic was such an enveloping experience that by being there one was inextricably involved with it, not just as an observer but as a participant. While I walked back down to the base with its lights sparkling in the growing dusk, the sounds of the huskies howling their night chorus wafted up from the dog spans. The howowooo sounded eerie as each call faded and another started in reply. It had been a very memorable evening, full of Antarctic character. Looking down at the buildings with the warm glow at the windows and then around at the panorama with its loneliness and deceptive calm, it made me thankful for the security of the base. It was a haven in an otherwise inhospitable place. The dusk blanketed the obvious hazards of the glaciers with their gaping crevasses, and the ice cliffs with their massive drops and teetering pinnacles. Despite my sad feelings of being apart from Sue, I enjoyed that walk enormously, not because it made me happy, for it did not, but because I was at peace. I was where God wanted me to be for reasons which I did not know nor was to know for some considerable time. I just knew that being there was right.

The next day we heard that the weather had manked* in close to my research area some 350 miles further south on George VI Ice Shelf*. One of the field parties which had flown out the day before had arrived at Fossil Bluff, a small hut which served as a summer-only air facility from which meteorological observations (met. obs.) could be radioed back to base to help plan the flying program. They had reported low cloud at the Bluff so there was no point in us even attempting to fly south. As I was to have at least one more day on base, I became involved in a work party in the Cold Room area of the 'Potting Shed'. This outbuilding had cost over a quarter of a million pounds and provided laboratories, workshops, storage for field gear and two large walk-in cold rooms. It seemed rather like taking coals to Newcastle to take cold rooms and refrigerators to the Antarctic. However, they were very necessary to store the frozen meat at a constantly cold enough temperature to ensure a good supply all year around. During the summer the temperature at Rothera could reach several degrees above freezing. Some of the large chest freezers were needed to keep ice samples at −20°C for scientific reasons; it was crucial that these specimens were not allowed to reach their melting point. This made us glaciologists feel that geologists had it easy as their samples were in no danger of ever melting.

My job for the day was to help paint the walls of the cold room area and to brighten up what were otherwise plain wooden wall boards. During morning smokoh, Bambi and Thumper were allowed into the scradge palace. They spent most of the time chasing each other around the table and chairs as fast as they could. However, they had great difficulty in controlling their legs as they rounded corners at speed since the floor was of lino and their paws would not grip. For us watching it was hilarious as they spun through 360 degrees or found their legs sliding out in four very different directions, ending up with their chins on the floor. Their only respite was to puddle or to mess before carrying on. If anyone's feet came into reach, a set of tiny but vicious teeth would set about the boot laces until the other pup pounced and the two disappeared locked in mock combat amidst chair legs. At the end of smokoh both pups were treated to a bowl of cold tea each which they lapped up greedily. In the absence of women, it seemed that the men's affection was turned to caring for the dogs.

That night I slept badly as one of my room mates snored loudly for what seemed all night. I was glad to have to be up in time to see that everything was ready for breakfast as I was on gash duty with one other Fid. After the meal came the washing up, then all the housework. By the end of the day I and my fellow gash man, Jerry, were worn out and ready to sit down in a comfy chair in the lounge to watch a film with everyone else. What made film watching on base more enjoyable was not the film itself, but the Fid reactions to the film as it was being screened. There was a constant banter either mimicking a character or lampooning something. If a line was particularly memorable it found its way into ordinary conversation. The Pink Panther films with Peter Sellars as Inspector Clouseau were especially good for that. Some of the overwinterers had seen the films so many times that they knew the script almost by heart. At smokoh, occasionally there would be an impromptu rendering of a scene with true Fid-overacting.

The following morning one of the pilots decided that the weather was sufficiently fine to try to fly us to our research area via Fossil Bluff. With all our gear packed we trundled up the airstrip on a snow-cat. The weather was not marvellous but it was good enough to see quite a way, so off we went. We reached to within 100 miles of the Bluff when we encountered thick low cloud as far south as we could see. There was a fair bit of turbulence as well. We aborted the flight and returned to Rothera. Intense frustration welled up. I felt angry at the weather for denying me my chance to start my research. I was becoming increasingly fed up with just filling in time on base when I should have been out in the field on the work I was supposed to be doing and for which I was paid.

I felt really down and the time dragged by. I tried writing to my parents but I could not think of much to say; I was not in the right frame of mind for that. I wandered down to see Bambi and Thumper. I fell to reading in the library, scanning snippets of books which took my fancy, such as *Humorous Quotations* which I found very unamusing. The sky matched my mood, overcast with gloomy prospects. In the early evening I listened to the Goon Show* with the sledge parties in the field to hear how they were faring. Each field party was allocated a sledge call sign for the radio schedule. Every evening Rothera would contact each party in turn to relay news. The base radio operator called the first sledge party up. The radio crackled as snow flurries outside set up interference. Faintly a reply was heard: 'Rothera, Rothera, Rothera. This is Sledge Delta. We receive you strength 1, strength 1. How are you doing, Flo'?'. Flo's real name was Lawrence but he had been renamed on base after a character called Florence from *The Magic Roundabout*. Flo' passed on his news and asked for theirs. They had found some scientific equipment which had been installed in the field during the previous season but it was completely iced up. Sledge Lima reported a nose ski had broken off one of their two skidoos so they had logistical problems and needed a spare part so their work was being delayed. And so it went on. The only sledge party not to report any bad news was Sledge Oscar. This was hardly surprising as that was my call sign and I was still firmly stuck on base. Because we were on constant standby, I could not really get stuck into any one particular activitiy just in case we had to rev* at a moment's notice. With all this bitty time on my hands punctuated only by meals and smokohs, my mind seemed quite happy to think of nothing in particular. I had a real case of Rothera lassitude. I went for walks, took photographs, wrote letters and listened to records and tapes. At least I had scradge to look forward to.

Sunday morning arrived accompanied by more snow. As there was no flying, I felt at least this Sunday was going to be a day of rest. My thoughts turned to home around 10.30 am as that was about the time that folk would be setting off for their respective church services, my mother to Falmouth and Sue and her family to our church in Bromley. I wondered whether Sue was thinking of me and what she really felt for me. Not having had any letters from her I could only speculate. I warmed to the memory of our fond 'goodbye'. Then I felt silly for letting such thoughts assume such importance. In the end I came to the same conclusion that I always arrived at, that trying to analyse our relationship was fraught with pitfalls into which, knowing myself, I would always fall. So at that point I tried to think about something else, which was not at all easy. I distracted myself by chatting to some colleagues about our reasons for coming south. Their answers were as varied as the people themselves. Some had read of Antarctic exploration when they were impressionable teenagers and so, for them this was a dream come true. Another said that his relationship with 'his woman' was becoming too serious for comfort. Another felt that he wanted to travel while he was free of family responsibilities and to see something of the world. Then there were those who wanted to combine visiting the Antarctic with their scientific research interests, whereas for myself, it was the other way around.

On Monday, shortly after lunch, the weather improved. Several of us took four skidoos up to the airstrip and bundled into the Twotter. We took off but somehow I knew that it would be another aborted attempt. We flew at only 1000 feet all the way until we reached the same point as on the last aborted journey. I was a case of *deja vu* although this was no illusion; it was a repeat. Mank was on the deck as far south as we could see. We circled several times to see if there was any way through the cloud bank, but it was to no avail. Mission aborted; back to Rothera. I was really cheesed off, not only by the fact that we had failed to get through this time but because my GA was blaming me for revving too hard to be flown into the field. I did not know whether he was winding me up as a joke or whether his comments were tinged with truth. I was cross as well as disappointed. By the time we had returned to base, dinner was long over, but some kind souls had kept us some food after they heard from Flo' of the abort. I found it very hard not to feel depressed and I tried hard to be as amused as everyone else at all the goings on. I tumbled into my pit* tired and depressed. I felt I needed to be able to share how I was feeling with someone who actually cared for me as a person, rather than just as a Fid like everyone else on base. I needed to talk out my depression, to remove it from my system. Oh why did I bother travelling all that way? Was I really in the right place? What had God in mind when He decided I should come to Rothera? I could see no purpose in it. If I had not joined BAS I could have been with Sue in Bromley. This was defeatist talk and I knew it, but I was too tired to care. With a jumble of thoughts in my mind I drifted off into a restless sleep.

The following morning was somewhat more exciting. We heard the news that an Antarctic cruise liner had run aground near Damoy. It seemed ironic to us that she had been chartered by a Japanese film company to make a film about a cruise liner running aground in the Antarctic. I am sure they found the story line closer to reality than they had anticipated. Apparently her starboard engine room had flooded and she had developed a 5 degree list. *Pilato Pardo*, a Chilean ice breaker was on her way to rescue the passengers, and a Swedish tug was to try to salvage the vessel. The initial reaction from the lads on base was one of glee, hoping that all the beautiful hostesses would be airlifted to Rothera but, alas, it was not to be. We found out that the ship's propeller tubes had been flooded and to complicate matters, the weather was worsening. The liner had requested Rothera to maintain a radio watch in case their situation deteriorated further and they needed to call for help.

As for me, I was beinning to feel that I was never going to do any research this season and so started to adjust mentally to that way of thinking. As a consequence I became more philosophical and began to take a renewed interest in what was going on around me.

By this time I was also finding that I was missing Sue far more than my own family. I really hoped that our relationship would develop with time, yet, I thought, what does the Lord want for her? There I was almost demanding of God that He should answer my prayers in the way that I wanted, rather than in accordance with His will. I tried to reconcile my own desires with less selfish reasons. If she was to be employed as a musician and spend her time travelling around, then our relationship was likely to peter out, I surmised. Alternatively, if she was to have a more settled and static job, then perhaps . . . It would be more than I could have hoped for if she was to find a job in Cambridge. I was learning to leave such matters in the Lord's hands and not to worry about them. I realised that I was holding on to everything which I was experiencing at that time and that I was not prepared to release any of it to the Lord. It was as true of my relationship with Sue as it was of my aborted flights south. Once I had grasped that fact, a weight lifted off my shoulders and I felt God say to me 'At last the penny was dropped!' and I felt daft. All the time I had the means of ending my feelings of depression by praying it all over to God and I, through my obstinacy, blindness and pride, would not. What a fool I had been. Perhaps that was what many other people back home did as well. Maybe they too, like me, refused to pray the right things because they thought they knew better than God. Their prayers were certainly answered, but they were not prepared to accept a 'no'.

Next day the news filtered through that a Russian tug was also bound for the listing liner but only had navigational charts as far south as Anvers Island. Rothera was radioed for instructions as to how to reach the grounded vessel. However, the Russian tug was too small to do much to help. The cruise ship was in danger of slipping off the rocks on which she was grounded and sinking, as the wind was starting to gust strongly. The *Pilato Prado* was also eager to return to port as with all the passengers on board she was running out of drinking water, but she could not leave until the Swedish tug had arrived from Santa Cruz.

The weather was showing signs of improving and Peter and I were put on two-hour standby. In my new frame of mind I was not concerned as I still had doubts as to whether I would ever reach the field so I stayed reading in the lounge. Two hours passed by and no flight. Suddenly, Rex, one of the pilots, came bustling through to say that we were off – all systems green. I turned back to my book. Most of us thought he was joking. He looked a bit taken aback by the non-response and had to convince us that we were supposed to rev. In ten minutes, we were on our way up to the airstrip. After digging out the aircraft we took off. Each of us was in exactly the same position as on the previous two flights. We half expected to fly no further south than before, but the landmark came and went. We really were going to make it. Any sense of tiredness I had a few moments before had vanished. We were going into the field; I had to keep on telling myself in order to believe it. We reached the Bluff very quickly and deliberately overflew it to try to locate the point on George VI Ice Shelf where I hoped to begin my research. Some years previously a set of metal poles had been erected across the ice shelf in order to monitor its behaviour – its movement and how much snow fell on it. I had planned to spend the first few weeks at the western end of this stake scheme, but first we had to find the poles. We failed to see any flags or poles from the air so our pilot landed on a slight rise in the shelf. With the engines still running we busily unloaded the aircraft of the first batch of gear. We clambered back on board and flew to Fossil Bluff to load the remaining gear. With all our kit, we returned to our depot on the ice shelf and unloaded everything else. In a matter of minutes everything was completed and all that remained to be done was to say cheerio and to look forward to seeing the plane again in a few weeks' time. The red fuselage of the Twotter glinted in the low-angled sunlight. Peter and I watched the plane disappear northwards until all that could be seen was a tiny black dot against the blue dusk sky.

So much for my relaxing evening in the base lounge! We

were some 40 miles south of Fossil Bluff standing on a featureless ice shelf equivalent in area to approximately half that of the English Channel. All we had for company were two skidoos, two sledges and masses of boxes. To the north and south we could see nothing but flat ice shelf. To the east we could make out some of the peaks of the Batterbee Mountains which marked the western edge of the mainland of the Antarctic Peninsula. To the west and considerably closer to us were the impressive stratified nunataks of eastern Alexander Island. What impressed me most at that time was that, contrary to all expectations, I did not feel isolated, but instead I was greatly excited at the prospect of starting work. After so many weeks of travellng, of disappointments, frustrations, and delays I was finally there. Thank God.

5: The Sound of Ice

Our first job on the ice shelf was to pitch our tent for the night. As I was the novice in Antarctic field craft, Peter's know-how helped enormously. In minutes, our orange pyramid-shaped tent was up. The skirt of the tent was weighted down with sledging boxes, jerry cans of fuel and boxes of equipment. Peter took on the role of 'outside man' and arranged the sledges and equipment so that nothing would blow away or be damaged in high winds. After all, we were totally dependent on ourselves and every piece of kit was necessary not just for comfort but for survival. I was 'inside man' and my job was to arrange the inside of the tent. I inflated our two airbeds and covered them with sheepskins. These were to provide insulation and to stop our body heat from melting the snow that supported us. Sleeping bags went on top of the fleeces. One manfood* box was placed crosswise between the two airbeds, another was placed next to the tunnel entrance to provide a step. The rectangular space in between the airbeds and boxes was sufficient for our primus stove. Suspended from the apex of the pyramid was a Tilley lamp which gave out considerable heat as well as light. Peter cut some snow blocks for our water and placed them between the two layers of the tent beside the entrance. With practice, the whole procedure could be completed within 15 minutes, but in very bad weather even that can seem a very long time.

After Peter had finished off outside, I fired up the primus stove for a brew and so began our first night on ice that season. It was surprisingly warm. With all the frantic activity of the previous few hours, it did not take long to drift off to sleep.

The peace of the night was shattered by Peter's alarm clock. We breakfasted on the standard field rations of porridge and hot sweet tea and struck camp and loaded up the sledges. We had to find that elusive marker pole so that we could set up our camp properly and start the research work. This was the first time that I had had to dress fully in all my cold-weather gear. Over my normal field clothes, I wore my windproof sledging jacket and trousers, large orange sledging boots called onitsukas, balaclava, goggles to cut down glare and protect my eyes from the cold and thick leather mittens called 'bear paws'. The name was derived from the pad of sheepskin attached to the back of the gloves which was used for wiping one's nose! It saved the palaver of digging into pockets for a handkerchief!

We started up the 'doos and sat until the engines had warmed sufficiently. Peter led the way and I followed in his tracks. I thumbed the throttle and the 'doo's caterpillar tracks bit into the snow. We were moving. The rope between my 'doo and the sledge pulled tight and I lurched as the 'doo took the strain of the weight of the sledge behind. The roar of the engines swamped every other noise. The vehicles moved swiftly over the smooth snow surface as we headed northwards to within about five miles of the western edge of the ice shelf, where the surface became much rougher and more difficult to traverse. Snow had formed hollows and concrete-hard ridges over which we had to travel very carefully. Despite our care, the front bridge on Peter's sledge split and the runners splayed apart. We stopped and unloaded it and made a depot which we marked with flagged poles. We rechecked our position and found that we were too far west; we had almost passed by the western end of the stake scheme without seeing any sign of flags. We did not even know if the markers set up those years ago had survived. Nevertheless, we set off on a bearing to the east towing one laden sledge, having left the broken one at the temporary depot. Suddenly Peter veered off sharply; he had seen a flag. A few minutes later we found Stake Number 1 of which only the top eighteen inches were visible above the snow. If we had been a year later, none of it would have been visible. We were exactly on target and could set about establishing our camp, with our accommodation tent and another pyramid tent which I was to use as my laboratory. Peter 'dooed back to our temporary depot to retrieve the remaining gear and the broken sledge while I put up the work tent on my own.

The first afternoon on site was spent unpacking and sorting out my scientific equipment in the work tent. I assembled everything into quite a comfortable and organised laboratory. One half of the tent was taken up with three manfood boxes providing a base for the very costly electronic equipment stacked on top. There were dials and knobs, wires and connectors, tools and notebooks all ready for use. The other half of the tent gave me room to sit as well as a place to store other scientific equipment. By dinner time I had tested most of the equipment. As far as I could tell, everything was fine.

That evening I cooked dinner. The steam from the pot rose through the tent and passed through a ventilator pipe at the top. Outside, the pipe pointed downwards so that snow (or rain) would not get into the tent. During cooking, steam would condense at the lower end of the pipe and form icicles. The danger for which we had to be on our guard was for this pipe to become iced up. If that happened, odourless carbon monoxide fumes from the stove would have accumulated in the tent with ultimately fatal consequences. When the ventilation pipe was working well, it looked like a small chimney from the outside and the whole tent was not too dissimilar from an Indian tepee. We remembered to take our vitamin pills with our meals— without them our diet would be deficient and our health would suffer. The commonest ailment was mouth ulcers. Our rations and diet had been evolved by BAS over 40 years of experience in the Antarctic. It provided several thousand calories each day which were necessary for the body to fight off the cold as well as to provide energy for physical work. The food was mostly dehydrated. It was fairly bland and most field men took with them packets of spices and herbs to add flavour. There was no fresh food at all within the manfood boxes; in fact the provisions when stored carefully could last for decades. A couple of our boxes had been made up in 1965 but everything inside was still perfectly edible. One daily treat was our individual bar of chocolate. This one luxury perked us up enormously. Each manfood box was designed to provide enough food for two men for ten days. Cooking manfood rations was an art and required ingenuity to try to dress up each meal into something better and more flavoursome than the last. It provided a good diversion from the pressures of work and helped alleviate boredom. Experienced field men also tried to have a manfood box of goodies* picked from base supplies with the cook's assistance. A tin of golden syrup for the breakfast porridge was a good choice (unless one was a Scot in which case such a selection was a heresy and extra salt was taken instead). Perhaps a tin of fruit, condensed milk, powdered egg and extra dried potato. Jams and other sandwich spreads provided relief from the ration of yeast extract. I was surprised that as the season progressed my sensitivity to the saltiness of yeast extract decreased. At the start of the season, only a thin veneer of the brown paste was sufficient. By the end I was caking the stuff on!

With the air being so dry, it was easy to become dehydrated. Tea bags were rationed and it took about twenty minutes to melt sufficient snow for a brew, so that often one went thirsty. Most men lost weight through the loss of water. I lost over seven pounds in as many weeks.

After we had completed our meal and tidied up it was

time for the Goon Show*. We had to report our new position and our progress. We switched on the radio and the crackle of the loudspeaker filled the tent. Communications (comms.) were not good, Flo's voice sounding distorted over the air but it was a comfort to know that we had a contact with the outside world and we listened as best we could to the news of other sledge parties. Later that evening, Flo' broadcast a New Year's Eve Request Show. Unfortunately comms. had worsened and all we could hear were snippets of *The Seekers Live* album sandwiched between Scottish music, bagpipes and drums, reels and marches, which faded and loomed irregularly. We switched off not long into the broadcast as we found it hard trying to distinguish between what we thought was music and the interfering crackle.

The remainder of the day, as with most days in the field, was spent writing up my scientific notes and my daily log. Often all this would take hours and sometimes was not finished until after midnight.

Having breakfasted well on the usual porridge, we began to assemble the long string of cables which were to connect to my equipment in the work tent. They stretched for nearly 430 yards each side of the work tent and had to be suspended from bamboo poles to stop the black wires from melting and later freezing into the snow. It took all day to assemble the array and install electrodes at the appropriate places at the ends of the wires.

The following couple of days were spent carrying out more tests on the system, refamiliarising myself with the equipment which I had not seen for over five months. I had to decide whether my results were realistic or if they were due to poor adjustment of my equipment. Sometimes the values I was obtaining were far too high to be reasonable and, at other times, far too low. The experiment was not as straightforward as I had anticipated. I was making silly mistakes and my mind wandered as I became increasingly cold. Sitting still inside the work tent just twiddling knobs and noting down numbers did not generate much heat. With my feet static on the groundsheet the cold worked its way up my body. First my feet went numb, then my ankles and knees. Even by rubbing my extremeties, the chill stayed until I went out of the tent and walked around for a few minutes to regain my blood circulation. The cold was not painful but was sufficiently uncomfortable to distract me from my work. In time I found ways to combat the rising cold using padded mats and improvised knee warmers. Yet when the sun was shining, the inside of the tent became like an oven. Layer after layer was peeled off in order to cool my top half, yet at the same time my lower limbs would be aching with cold. I felt like the proverbial statistican who, with his feet in an ice box and his head in a hot oven, said that on average he felt fine! I often had to fight to retain my concentration. The trouble was that in order to perform the experiment I had to make repetitive observations and measurements, day in and day out. The apparent lack of progress was demoralising and made it difficult to concentrate on the tasks in hand. But time was passing by and I was under growing pressure to complete all my planned research within the time allotted.

While I was absorbed in my experimental work, Peter was digging pits in the snow to help me find out what layering there was in the top few feet of the ice shelf. At about five feet down he encountered water, ponded between lenses of ice. One pit not far from our living tent provided us with an easy supply of fresh water, so fresh that it was purer than distilled water. This saved us fuel and time as it reduced the necessity to melt snowblocks. Peter also visited some of the other poles of the nearby stake scheme to measure how much of each pole was still exposed above the snow surface. By repeating these measurements during our field work we could monitor how much snow had fallen and melted. This was all part of our work to try to understand the physical processes that enabled the ice shelf to survive.

After one particularly depressing day where nothing seemed to go right, both Peter and I were feeling distinctly gloomy. After a very nondescript dinner we tuned in to the Goon Show as normal. After the usual exchanges between the various sledge parties and Rothera, we were called up again. There was an air letter for each of us which Flo' read out over the air. Air letters enable family and girl friends to send radio messages from home to their menfolk in the field. Each man was allowed to receive 200 words a month and in turn to send out the same amount. I had asked my parents to send 100 words a month and Sue to do the same. When Flo' did not say who my air letter was from, I immediately hoped and prayed that it was from Sue. I needed to hear from her to know how things stood between us. Air letters did not permit intimacy as not only could we hear what was being broadcast, but every other person in the whole of the Antarctic Peninsula too! We knew that it was likely some of my colleagues were listening in on the off-chance of some gossip so as soon as 'Flo said that it had been sent by Sue, I could almost hear the ears around the peninsula fluttering, and radios being fine tuned for better reception. Messages from girl friends were a great source of discussion. The fun in listening in to them was to identify comments which could, perhaps, have more intimate interpretations. Normally it was just innocent fun. I listened intently as Flo' read out Sue's message, enjoying every word. The things she said meant a great deal to me and even a long time afterwards I mulled over her air letter. I knew then that I was not forgotten, that she had been thinking about me and perhaps would be waiting for me on my return. The receipt of that message triggered off all sorts of thoughts in my mind about our relationship. I started to read into her sentences hidden meanings, which was an unwise thing to have done. Peter's air letter was from his girlfriend so both our morale had been raised enormously. As a consequence, Peter and I seemed to get on more freely than before. With the more relaxed atmosphere in the tent, my perception of my situation changed and I decided that I was really enjoying life in the field.

One afternoon I heard the sound of a skidoo approaching. Thinking it was just Peter checking our vehicles, I continued beavering away in my work tent. Suddenly, the flap over the tent entrance parted and a head appeared. We had visitors. Tim, the plant fossil geologist, and his GA, Clive, were en route to a location called Coal Nunatak, which was some forty miles south of us. They thought they would drop in for a cup of tea as they were passing. It was a delightful surprise, especially as Peter and I had not been expecting to see other human faces for several more weeks. Tim and I nattered away about our respective research while Clive and Peter chatted in the living tent. After Tim and Clive had driven off I returned to the work tent to test out some more ideas, which were not successful. The weather was starting to worsen and what had been a slight breeze during that morning had developed into a strong wind with occasional gusts which rocked the tent and howled through the guy lines. Flurries of drifting snow drummed against the taut outer fabric and we were glad to be snug inside the tent and well out of the weather.

That night was long and sleepless. The wind became strong and relentless and by breakfast time it was up to fifty knots with severe ground drift and blowing snow. My lines of bamboo canes were taking a hammering. At one point I poked my head through the tunnel entrance of the tent to survey the scene and wished I had not bothered. The canes were bowed and bent as the wind tried to force them to the ground. I saw two adjacent canes snap and tens of yards of cable were engulfed in the snow. The sky was clouded over and I could see only the base of the nearby mountains, their tops being completely shrouded in swirling mists. I was not going to complete any work which involved the cables that day. Instead Peter and I went out to one of the pits to take snow samples for later analysis. Whilst down in the pit the wind-driven snow flew over us. When I stood up to climb out the coarse abrasive ice grains struck me full in the face. The blast was blinding and painful. We were pleased to find respite back in the living tent a few moments later, our ruddy faces continuing to tingle from the onslaught of the weather outside. The sounds of the wind were temporarily masked by the hiss of the primus as we prepared a warming brew. We cupped our cold hands around the pan over the stove trying to restore the blood circulation in our fingers. The ice which had frozen into my beard gradually melted and my chin thawed out. When we supped our hot drinks we felt as if we were glowing; it was lovely. A fierce gust of wind rocked the whole tent as if to remind us of the strength of the elements outside. Peter and I looked at each other starkly. How much more buffeting could the tent withstand, I asked. Peter reassured me that as long as the outer canvas was intact, it could take considerably stronger winds. He added a warning caveat; coarse ice crystals blasted against canvas were as effective as sand blasting. The top of the tent where it was under the most stress would go first, closely followed by the sides. Once the wind had whipped inside, the remainder of the tent would only last seconds before being blown away completely along with the contents. There would be certain warning signs before that ultimate stage was reached and the occupants would hopefully have time to dress in their outdoor windproofs and climb into bivouac bags. However, if they were caught napping, their chances of survival would have been severely reduced, probably to zero. The smacking of the wind on the tent's outer skin was disconcerting but we were safe – for the moment.

I picked up the book I had started the evening before – *The New Wine is Better* by Robert Thom. The author's main theme was that in all things we should praise

God. I had tried that yesterday morning and my experiment worked better; I tried it again in the afternoon, and my experiment failed. Oh for the simple life! I was guilty of taking Thom's thesis and applying it as if it were my horoscope. How could I have relegated the power of Christ to mere superstition? I chided myself for my foolishness. If I was to glean the real truth behind what was being said in that book, I was going to have to think more deeply and more seriously. At least the book had made me think of the issues involved. I pondered over whether there was any purpose in me being there in the Antarctic. What had God in store for me, then or later? I questioned my motives for joining BAS and going south – had I done a Jonah and gone to my own Ninevah? So much seemed to have gone awry – the start to my season being delayed again and again, becoming icebound at Faraday and missing the first air relief from Damoy to Rothera, and now there were the far from ideal conditions in which my experiments were not working very well; it felt as if my season was jinxed. Was this God's way of telling me I was in the wrong place? Or was I in the right place, doing what I was supposed to be doing, but I was not atuned to it? I did not know nor was I in a position to find out straight away. There was no divine sign in the sky saying, 'John, you are in the right place – hang on in there.' I could only begin to know God's will by drawing closer to Christ through my prayer times and Bible reading. It was a process that took time, effort and faith on my part, and perseverance despite doubts, fears, and pessimism. I was there in the Antarctic and there was no going back; I had to resolve my situation and I had work to do; if I spent all my time worrying about spiritual rationale, I would never complete any experiment. I took Thom's advice and I praised God although I did not know the purpose, or the reasons behind my being there. I praised God for allowing me the privilege of experiencing one of the most unspoilt of all the continents on earth, and for being in a job where I could study God's world. Having done that, it did not take away the philosophical problems that I felt I was facing, but it equipped me so I could tackle them without fearing them.

The storm continued unabated well into the evening and I started reading another book, *The Happiest People on Earth* by Demos Shakarian. It told the autobiographical story of an Armenian dairyman and how through the workings of the Holy Spirit in his life, he founded the Full Gospel Business Men's Fellowship International so that Christian business people could share the Gospel with their colleagues. The book made me feel I was lacking so much in my Christian life, especially the baptism of the Holy Spirit. Perhaps that was why God wanted me to read that book so I would realise my many shortcomings. How did these folk in the book receive such clear-cut revelations from the Lord? Why did I not? It would have made such a difference to my way of life, I was sure. I knew that it was fairly easy to maintain an outward appearance as a Christian when within a regular Christian community. One could be buoyed up by one's friends and their outward faith, so that the very foundations of one's relationship with Christ could have been eroded without one realising it. The real test was when the group had been removed, isolating the individual. It was like someone who had relied on crutches for so long not realising that they could have walked on their own a long while previously. Had those crutches been removed sooner, that person would have known exactly when they were able to stand on their own two feet, perhaps wobbly at first perhaps with the occasional need for help from others to avoid falling, but still walking all the same. That was how I felt in my Christian life then. I was a long way from my home church, from the fellowship of my very good friends, from the corporate worship on Sundays. It had been easy to go to church, to say prayers, to sing the hymns and to be seen to be a Christian, yet inside I could have been thinking about anything but the service, and no one by me would know, no one, that is, but God. Humans, I thought, could be so good at acting that after a time they begin to believe their own act. By being thrust into an icy cold wilderness where there was no one for fellowship there could be no pretence, only the harsh reality of survival, physical, mental and spiritual. I was forced by my isolation to turn to the only one available for such matters, God himself. I realised that there I was sitting out a storm and God was waiting for me as if I was the only person in the whole world. He had time to listen; He understood me; He knew how I felt; He understood that I was only human. I felt as if I had been like a small child chasing around in a crowd confused when all that he could see was a bewildering muddle with no faces to recognise or friends with whom he could identify; growing increasingly frightened and alarmed; then a hand reached down and gently touched his shoulder and stopped him in his tracks. The child looked up and saw the face of his father, smiling and saying, 'Why are you so frightened? I've been here all the time beside you, only in your haste you haven't seen me. Stop and don't be so anxious.' I realised that there in that tent, God was teaching me a lesson, not of self-reliance but of reliance on him. So often I had been too busy with things around me to look into myself and see just how empty I was. On that ice shelf, I started to fill up again; I had been reassured that I was in the right place, and God was very much with me. God had said that just as I had checked over every component of my experiment to find the faulty part or wrong connection, I had to do the same thing with my own life. I had been reminded of Paul's message in his second letter to the Corinthians (chapter 13, verse 5) when he wrote: 'Put yourselves to the test and judge yourselves, to find out whether you are living in faith. Surely you know that Christ Jesus is in you? . . . ' The certainty of that last sentence spoke deeply to me. I had a new assurance. Despite the wind having increased to over sixty knots that night I felt easier. The deafening blast of the snow driving against the tent walls denied us sleep and the sudden shaking of the tent as if grasped by fearsome hands outside was still alarming. The passage of time that night was painfully slow, yet I knew we were not alone. I could feel the protection of God surrounding us. The next thing I remembered was waking up because of the quiet. The wind had stopped, snow no longer chafed the tent. It was gone 11 o'clock in the morning. I fought to untangle the tunnel entrance which had frozen up. The fabric was rigid and creaked as I prised apart the tapes that had tied the door shut. The cardboard-hard material gave slowly and a waft of cold air rushed into the tent along with a shower of snow from the flank of the tent. I crawled out to see the view. The tent was buried half way up to the top on the windward side with snowdrifts of three to four feet around the sides. The sledges had been engulfed; we could only tell where they were by the characteristic shape then taken on by the snow which covered them. My bamboo poles and cables had been decimated. The flags hung sadly from broken canes. Some bamboos had split open and collapsed, no longer able to take the strain of the wind beating against them. It was a depressing sight of devastation. It would take hours just to dig everything out, let alone resurrect the cable array, the wires of which lay buried deep beneath the snow. We set about the arduous task of shovelling tons of snow to relocate our equipment and to re-establish my experiment. The snow was wet and heavy and seemed to become heavier as the day wore on. By evening, the digging was complete but it took two days of repairs and modifications before I started to make progress with my scientific work again. But now, the data were starting to show a pattern. Gradually I felt the ice shelf was relinquishing its long-held secrets. The keen anticipation of discovery gave a new impetus to the research and I went to work excited at the prospect of what the new day's data were going to reveal. There were continued frustrations as I made mistakes, as I learned to alter my procedures to take into account the shifting conditions outside as I became more accustomed to working and living in that harsh environment, but at least progress was being made.

A few days later, after a hard day in the work tent, I suddenly realised that it was a Sunday. I would hardly have thought it from the day's activities. My thoughts turned to my friends at Bromley at the church which meant so much, and especially Sue. I was looking forward to seeing her again — it was only another twenty weeks or so to go. That evening, as I sat on a manfood box outside the tent door, I read Psalm 104 which seemed remarkably apt: 'You spread the heavens like a tent . . . You use the clouds as your chariot and ride on the wings of the wind . . . You have set the earth firmly on its foundations, and it will never be moved . . . May the glory of the Lord last for ever! May the Lord be happy with what he has made! . . . Praise the Lord!' The mountains of Alexander Island touched the base of the clouds which fleeted past northwards. The breeze from the south was cold but dry. The sun shone weakly over the icy realm. The view complemented the poetry of the Psalm beautifully.

Slowly the days passed by and the work progressed bit by bit. On some days I made major steps forward into my season's program and accomplished a great deal. On others, I was frustrated by bad weather or I was overtired and did not work as efficiently as I ought. The inside of our living tent was gradually taking on a new look too. As our camp had been static, the heat from our bodies and from the stove and tilley lamp had melted some of the snow in the centre of our groundsheet. We were effectively living on a saucer shaped floor, with the centre being almost nine inches below the perimeter. Consequently things tended to gravitate towards the middle. The stove was much lower than when we started and we were in danger of toppling off our airbeds during the night and ending up on the cold floor. To remedy this Peter emptied the tent of its contents including the groundsheet and shovelled snow from the outside into the tent. He then compacted this new snow and levelled it to provide a firm flat base on which we could live without discomfort.

Apart from my main experiments I was also interested in examining where the ice shelf impinged against the contra-flowing glaciers of eastern Alexander Island. As daytime travel was proving difficult because of slushy soft snow, we decided to travel at night to take advantage of the crisper surface. Peter and I set off with just our skidoos which carried all the supplies we needed for the trip. After twenty minutes of fast motoring we reached an area covered in pools of water. We had no way of knowing how deep these ponds were; they could have been only inches or many feet deep. They were covered over by ice which in its turn was partially obscured by fresh snow. We had to drive carefully and slowly so as to avoid being engulfed in one of the pools. The ice shelf at this point cambered steeply westwards towards the shore of Alexander Island. We could see the land-based glaciers flowing down toward us from the mountains. We carried on with the 'doos as far as we could. Our way was barred by a wall of ice some thirty feet high which had been caused by the immense pressure of the ice shelf meeting the much thinner glacier ice moving in the opposite direction. The ice had become corrugated through compression. These huge pressure ridges provided a formidable obstacle. We decided to go the rest of the way by foot. Peter and I roped together for safety. We clambered up the nearest ice ridge to try to see beyond. On the way up I found some ice crystals which were between fifteen and twenty inches in length and the clear ice was so brittle that when tapped they sounded like fragile glass. The crystals were slightly curved along their length making them more like sabres. Right the way through the middle of each crystal was a hollow tube making these crystals natural drinking straws. The only trouble with them was trying to climb over them. Because they were so friable, they collapsed whenever any weight was put on them, with the broken crystals cascading down in a tinkling avalanche. We reached the top and surveyed the scene. There were rows of near-parallel pressure ridges between which deep lakes of turquoise melt-pools drained into holes in the ice. Some of the ice was covered in a sprinkling of wind-blown dirt from the nearby rock cliffs and moraines. The melt-pools were far too wide and deep for us even to contemplate crossing. We managed to circumnavigate several, each time walking westwards and closer to the mountains of Alexander Island. To the south west of us we could clearly discern the shape of Two Step Cliffs, whose name described the tiers of the rocky crag very well. We were almost at the foot of the next set of crags north of Two Step Cliffs, at a place called Ares Cliff. The surface underfoot consisted of loose grains of dry ice, with each grain being about one third of an inch across. It was like walking across marbles. Occasionally we encountered streams incised into the glacier surface. Some channels were sufficiently small that we could simply step over them. Others were more substantial, perhaps as deep as a man is tall, and too wide to jump across unaided. We had with us a bog-chisel* with a handle about five feet long. By placing that in the middle of the stream and pole-vaulting across we could just make the other side. Fortunately, we managed to cross all the streams without mishap. After several hours we found our way barred by a huge melt-water lake. Facing us on the other shore was an impressive moraine which exposed its ice core. I was keen to try to find a way to examine this feature in more detail, but there was no way that we could have crossed that lake, except by boat. I found some moraine on our side of the water and so we were able to spend some time examining the rock fragments there. I found some very well preserved plant fossils looking like tropical fern leaves which I bagged for later identification and some small pieces of coal. High up on the cliff I could make out a thin, near horizontal black band which I assumed must have been from where the samples had originated. What a paradox – tropical flora in a continent in the grip of an ice age. This apparent enigma had a fantastic story to tell; of how, many millions of years ago, the whole area where I was standing had been where Africa is today – in the tropics. Indeed the flora had consisted of lush plants and trees. Not far north from us, Tim Jefferson (the geologist who had visited our camp earlier in the season) had found a fossil forest with tree stumps still in place. The coal had formed from rotten vegetation just as it had formed in Britain, America, and elsewhere in Antarctica where massive coal deposits are known to exist throughout the Trans-Antarctic Mountains. Since those early days of heat the continent itself had drifted southwards to its present position, just as the continents of America and Europe had drifted apart. How could I reconcile this with what had been written in Genesis chapter 1? So much had been written in Christian literature about fundamentalism and the necessity of a belief in the absolute literalism of the Scriptures. This so-called clash between the subject in which I had trained and the supposed scientific and theological objections raised by fundamentalists was not new to me. I had had many years over which to think, read and pray my own way through this issue. Many years before, I had been an ardent 'creationist' and had hotly disputed any argument that expressed opposition. Slowly with my increasing interest in geology I began to read what the geologists were saying, and travelled around Europe and Scandinavia and made my own observations. During my Antarctic voyage I had seen that while the beginning of Genesis provides the *theological* reason for the existence of the Universe and the development of Mankind, it does not provide a *scientific* treatise, for scientific knowledge is temporal. Genesis is for all times, all people everywhere. Genesis chapter 1 was for me like the abstract of a scientific paper: giving the conclusions and the most important points. The 'creation story' was for me true in concept. It was not like a divine magician conjuring up his *pièce de résistance* in a puff of smoke and a swish of his magic wand. Rather, it was like a master painter building up his picture on his canvas stroke by stroke. The finished piece was the picture which was in the painter's mind at the outset. He knew what he wanted to portray but it took time. That was how I envisaged God creating the world, by creating the laws of nature that would develop a natural and a beautiful world for the ultimate creation, man. For me, the geological arguments did not detract from the scriptures nor weaken their meaning but did the opposite. How much more powerful and omniscient must our Creator be to have known how to achieve His objective over such an enormous timespan, some 4,500 million years? How much more awesome He was to me for having created all this, and yet have time for me? Whenever I pondered over this thought it caused me a sense of amazement and enormous gratitude to Him.

I packed my fossils carefully for the return journey from the moraine back to our vehicles and then we set off roped together. We had crossed nearly all the pressure ridges when, suddenly, Peter crashed through a weak ice bridge when descending down the flank of a ridge made largely from candle ice. Peter was up to his arms, and his legs dangled into what appeared to be a grotto with cold blue water below. Fortunately, it did not take long to extricate Peter from his predicament, but he had dropped our bog chisel into the water. We could just make out the chisel's handle as it bobbed up and down in the pool below. To avoid jeopardising our own safety we decided to dig sideways down into the grotto so we did not have to put our weight on the feeble ice bridge again. After several attempts we retrieved the chisel without further ado and we were soon back at our 'doos which we loaded up and then motored back to our tents. We arrived back at camp nearly an hour later, having picked our way carefully through the melt-pools. It was by then almost dawn. We were exhausted after what had been a most rewarding scientific trip, as well as having been a somewhat exciting excursion.

We had virtually completed our work at the camp site so we set about preparing to move on to our next destination some eleven miles to the east. While we were taking down the array of cables and canes the weather was fine and warm with the sun bearing down on us. We worked shirtless and within minutes my torso tingled with the effect of the sun. Soon all the gear was neatly tidied up and lashed to the sledges. All that remained was to wait until nightfall and the harder snow surface before travelling.

At 11.30 pm we struck camp and completed loading our sledges. As we sat idling the 'doo engines to warm them up, we watched the beautiful sun low in the southern sky. Several irridescent clouds looked like giant pearls with the blend of colours that is normally associated with mother of pearl. Ice crystals on the ice shelf surface sparkled in the sunlight like a myriad of diamonds. We set off eastwards over the crisp ice to find our next set of stakes. By about 3 am we found the stake and established our new camp. We were about to embark on the next stage of the season's research. Tiredness was tinged with excitement as I wondered what this new site would reveal.

6: The Goodenough Camp

Our new camp site was on the Goodenough Glacier which was one of the major tributaries of the ice shelf. Up on the Antarctic Peninsula plateau the glacier was over 5000 feet thick. The ice flowed down towards George VI Sound to the west where it went afloat. We were some seventeen miles west of the coast of the peninsula and our camp moved westwards with the ice three feet or more a day. The glacier in its entirety was nearly eighty miles long and some twenty-five miles wide. It was thought that this mammoth flow of ice had been in existence for at least several thousand years. Our task was to investigate its structure.

After only four hours of sleep we started to erect the array of cables and bamboo canes. The snow was soft underfoot which made walking very tiring, but in the fine weather it was possible to work quite fast and by late afternoon the array was completed and ready to be tested.

After dinner, I decided that salt solution was needed in the snow around each electrode in order to make better electrical contact between the electrodes and the ice shelf. Peter melted the snow and made up billies of the solution whilst I skied along the array carrying a billy at a time, trying not to slop too much over the sides. Unbeknown to me, on one journey along the array to one of the most distant electrodes, I had my right thumb in the salt solution. Whilst skiing back with the empty billy, the thumb had become frost-nipped. The tip of my thumb was completely white and was frozen hard. I could not feel a thing. I nursed it trying to re-establish the blood circulation which did eventually and very painfully return. For the following ten days, that thumb was over-sensitive and even the slightest touch sent shivers of pain racing through my arm and down my back. It made trying to work and write very difficult. In addition to the frost-nip, the day out in the sun had left me with badly sunburnt neck and face, and my lips had swollen, becoming blistered and cracked. Each time I smiled the cracks would reopen and bleed. I was in considerable physical discomfort.

Next morning the weather was cold and miserable but matched our moods. Over breakfast Peter was uptight about something and hardly spoke. It made me feel wary in case I said something out of place. The atmosphere in that tent was tense, and I was glad to have the excuse of having to go to the work tent to continue with my experiments. Fortunately by lunch time, whatever it was that was bugging Peter had passed and he was more cheerful.

That evening, as we sat in our tent slurping our runny meat munch and powdered potato, we thought we heard a very distinctive hum which sounded just like a Twotter several miles away. I crawled out of the tent to scan the skies but could see nothing. Peter had powered up the radio and was calling the aircraft, but there was no reply. After ten minutes or so we realised that the noise we had heard was no more than the sound of a slight breeze in a tight guy rope. We felt very disappointed as no plane meant no mail. We consoled ourselves with an extra bar of chocolate each and put it down to experience.

Each day passed by in much the same way. Breakfast of porridge and tea, work on experiments with a short break for biscuits and tea at lunch time, then dinner of tasteless munch, followed by radio sched, then more work writing up the day's results and preparing for the next day. We had several bad blows which caused us to lie up for a day or so. If the work went well morale was fair; if it did not, then frustration and depression were the order of the day.

One evening at the radio sched we were told that a plane would be en route to us the following day. This news caused us great excitement as perhaps, this time, we would have some mail. Next morning we were on to the air to Rothera giving our weather report and all was dingle*. We were told the Twotter would be with us within three hours so we tidied up the camp in readiness for our visitors. The next thing we heard was a tremendous roar overhead. I rushed out of the tunnel entrance just in time to see the tail of a Twotter disappearing southwards. While it banked and circled, Peter contacted the pilot over the radio to inform him of the snow conditions on the ground and of any wind. When the Twotter came in again, low over the tent, the fierce draught from the two propellers whipped up the loose snow into a mini-blizzard. One ski touched down and the plane suddenly flipped heavily onto the opposite ski and the nose dipped sharply. The pilot had misjudged the gradient of the snow and the plane was about to cartwheel. The pilot applied more thrust to the engines and the plane roared skywards again. It circled then approached along a different tack and safely touched down. The Twotter taxied towards us and stopped only yards from the front of our tent. We rushed up to the aft door, took delivery of four manfood boxes and a mailbag and loaded onto the plane the gear which we wanted returned to Rothera. Within minutes the engines were started and the Twotter inched her way forward, taxied away from the tent, then took off effortlessly We watched the plane until it was only a tiny black speck in the sky. The faces of the air crew were the first we had seen for weeks, and they were gone again so soon. We opened up the manfood boxes to see what we had been sent. Two boxes were of ordinary rations and the other two contained goodies* – six beautiful red apples, two oranges, four onions, tins of corned beef, steaks, a jar of peanut butter, a loaf of bread, paté and a couple of other spreads. This was a great morale booster. Peter picked up the mail bag and began to sort out our post. The first item out was a large brown paper parcel for him but all the letters were for me; Christmas cards from my family and from my friends in London. It was great to find out how things were at home. The weather in England appeared to be worse than ours! We had been sent a bottle of port in the goodies box so we cracked it open and had a tipple along with a slice of fresh bread with peanut butter. What luxury! Peter's parcel had been a box of chocolates from a favourite aunt. That he had not received any letters or cards made me feel like giving him some of mine to open. In the goodies box Peter had been sent some books. One was *Punch on Scotland*, an hilarious character assassination of the Scots people which was all the funnier as Peter came from Edinburgh. But there was still the disappointment that there was no letter from Sue. I consoled myself with her Christmas card which I pinned to the inside of the tent above my sleeping bag. Despite this disappointment I just felt I had to thank the Lord. I did not know why or for what, but I thanked him all the same. After all, was that not what Paul had said in Ephesians 5 verse 20 – 'always give thanks for everything to God the Father.' It is always easy to say thank you for the good things, but when there are disappointments, failures, frustrations, pain and so on, to be thankful then is a major effort. I knew that whatever circumstances befell me, that God was in control and that he knew best for me. No matter where we were geographically, God was always near at hand, of that I was certain.

When the weather was bad it was uncomfortable and miserable but when it was fine it was beautiful, especially in the evening. Shadows were long and dark blue. The ice crystals on the ice shelf glistened like cut glass. The snow appeared a brilliant blue, not white. From where we were camped we could still see the nunataks on Alexander Island to the west, and to the east we could make out the great icefall of Goodenough Glacier.

One evening over the Goon Show, we were treated to the results of what was the greatest sporting event on Adelaide Island, the 'Rothera Mile' race. The circuit was around the base over the beach shingle which was far from ideal as a surface on which to race. The athletes who had been in training for at least the five minutes preceding the race were a real mixture of physique and fitness, from tall, lean and fairly fit to short, fat and totally unfit. However, the race was hotly contested and the winner turned out to be one of the GAs who had completed the distance in six minutes flat. However, the base was then littered with physical wrecks of exhausted Fids. As the season progressed so the Goon Show took on a more important social role amongst the sledge parties. After the official traffic had been passed, sledges could arrange to talk to each other over different channels as communication conditions allowed. Sometimes the chat was about the work, other times it was asking for advice or just banter about the weather. There were definitely days when the field Fids were in the mood for a witter* over the Goon Show, and also days when they were not. As the season progressed the frequency of such chitchat increased. However, battery power was an important resource and could not be wasted as the radio provided our only link with the outside world. If an accident had happened then that radio would have been absolutely vital. There was also a safety code that each sledge party was supposed to keep contact each day at the evening radio sched. If a sledge party was travelling then that was not possible. Base would not worry until they heard nothing for forty-eight hours. After that efforts would be made to raise the party to check on their safety. If several evening scheds were missed for no apparent reason, then the people on Base would become very anxious and a search and rescue operation might be instigated at the discretion of the Base Commander. It was the responsibility of each sledge party to ensure that Base knew its latest camp position. Each time we moved we had to inform Flo' of our new QTH, radio jargon for position. In the event of an emergency this would be the first place the plane would begin its search. It was a comfort to know that despite being so far from Base and so remote, our wellbeing was carefully looked after.

Over the same sched we heard that one of the planes had just returned from Port Stanley and had some more mail on board. I hoped that there would be a letter for me from Sue. This was worse than waiting for a letter at home; at least there one knew when the postman was going to arrive, but out on that ice shelf, we never knew when to expect anything.

Our work was progressing and we were on schedule for finishing everything by the end of the season if nothing went wrong. We still had two more moves to do. Our bodies were acclimatised to our physical conditions although we had painfully swollen and cracked lips despite the lipsalve cream. My ankles and wrists had developed mild rheumatism and ached from the cold and seemed as if they would never warm up. Working outside was fine in sunny weather. Poor weather was another case entirely. Writing notes was easy at first whilst hands still had full manual dexterity, but when the cold had set in, fingers became stiff and even holding a pencil, let alone writing with it, became a real task.

A couple of days later we were due for another visit by one of the planes in order to deliver our mail and several pieces of needed kit. When the Twotter arrived, it flew over the camp with a horrendous roar, then circled. We thought it was going to land, but quick visit it was indeed. The plane turned to approch the camp and flew at about ten feet from the surface. The side door of the plane opened slightly and a manfood box was kicked out and landed not far from one of our tents. The delivery made, the plane flew on to its next destination. We rushed over to the box and in our eagerness to see what was inside, opened it there and then.

Instead of the two small plastic bottles we had requested, there were two hundred which made Peter go off into a fit of swearing and shouting about the ineptitude of various people on base and within BAS in general. I left him to work it out of his system. I had made the mistake once before of trying to talk him out of it, but it only made matters worse. What did console him was a bundle of letters for us, some of which were for him from his girlfriend Joan. Amongst those for me was one which I recognised as being from Sue. The long-awaited letter had arrived at last. We bustled everything back into the manfood box and retired to the living tent.

The next couple of hours were spent reading our mail. Peter sat on his airbed reading his letters from Joan, occasionally quoting extracts for me. I opened Sue's letter and read it avidly, taking in each word, enjoying every syllable. I then opened a large plain brown envelope. Inside were a whole bundle of letters which had been written to 'The man at the South pole' by a class of nine-year-old girls from Roedean School, Brighton in Sussex. A friend of mine was a teacher at the school and she had given her class an exercise on the topic of snow and ice, part of which was to write to me. All the letters contained jokes and puzzles because the children obviously thought that I would have had nothing with which to occupy my time. The most popular topic for jokes was, inevitably, penguins: 'What goes black and white, black and white, black and white? A penguin rolling downhill!' Some of the children told me about the winter they were having in Brighton, or about their holidays. The letters were very cheery and were delightful to read.

Having been through all our correspondence several times over, it was back to work. It was necessary to extend the cable array out to nearly 1100 yards. Some of the wire which had been installed previously had by then melted down about six inches into the snow. We had to raise this wire before we could add any extensions. Peter drove one of the 'doos with me on the back holding a bamboo cane out to one side. At the far end of the cane we had tied a prussik loop* through which the cable ran. By motoring along by the frozen wire in this manner, the black strands of cable soon emerged from below. We had completed one side in no time at all and we were very pleased with this improvised method of working. However, on the other side of the array things went very badly wrong. Our new wonder method failed abysmally and the cable ended up in a complete mess. It was like trying to knit with half a mile of telephone wire. I became very cross as I fought with the wires trying to untangle them. The longer I struggled the crosser I became. For a while the air was blue as I swore in frustration and anger. I did not know what it was that fired me up so much, whether it was the mess the wires were in, or my ineptitude for allowing them to be so tangled or that this problem provided a trigger for the release of a lot of latent frustration with the work. Thankfully, once the cable was sorted out my better humour returned.

Peter and I spent the remainder of the evening chatting. As usual the topic was women. As we chatted the weather worsened with the wind growing stronger and the clouds closing in. During a lull in the wind it snowed ice spicules which looked very picturesque. Our conversation was accompanied for some of the time by music from my tape recorder. The recorder could only be used for a short while as the batteries soon ran down in the cold, turning Olivia Newton John's voice into a wowing bass.

The following evening the Goon Show was quite busy for Sledge Oscar. I had a telex message from Cambridge relayed to me which told me that a research paper of mine had been published in *Nature* along with a scientific critique I had written. The news of these publications heartened me enormously. I also heard that a cheque had arrived for another article I had written for *The*

Geographical Magazine. The successful broadcasting of my publications prompted one of the GAs in one of the other sledge parties to refer to me teasingly as 'Enid Blyton'. In attition to my telex, I received an air message from my father. It appeared that my father had left his job and was going to buy a general store in a small Cornish village and run it with the help of my mother. This was great news as my parents had been separated for over eighteen months. It was something that both my sister and I had been praying about. I was delighted. This was indeed a memorable Goon Show for me. After all the other traffic Sledge Golf patched in and requested a chat on Channel 12. We tuned in and found that their tape recorder had given up the ghost and they were musicless. Could we play some music over the air for them? We obliged as long as our tape recorder batteries permitted. I sat holding the radio handset to the loudspeaker of the tape recorder trying to hold the 'transmit' button down. Sledge Oscar had become 'Radio Oscar' and I had my only experience of being a disc jockey. The effort was much appreciated by Sledge Golf.

One very fine evening a couple of days later, Peter and I sat outside the tent having completed a good day's work. We felt replete and contented. The sun felt warm although the temperature was several degrees below zero. There was no wind and it was delightfully serene. In the evening colours the mountains of eastern Alexander Island could be seen miraged up into strange contorted images which changed as we watched them. The miraging effect enabled us to see for many tens of miles both north and south along George VI Sound, way north beyond Fossil Bluff, and far to the south of Coal Nunatak where Tim and Clive had been working. To the east was the icefall of Goodenough Glacier. Visibility was so good that we could make out the individual seracs* and mammoth crevasses which made the icefall so spectacular. The sight of that enormous glacier under those conditions to me as a glaciologist was fascinating and tremendously beautiful. Individual glaciers seem to have their own distinctive character which takes time to know. They can almost be described as having moods, of being active or passive, slow to react or fast, aggressive or peaceful. They have an aesthetic as well as a scientific attraction. I felt I needed to study them and it became almost a physical urge that had to be met.

One of the other apparent paradoxes on George VI Ice Shelf was that despite the cold and the wet, it was part of what was effectively the world's largest desert. Just as in a sandy desert there were sand dunes, there were snow dunes with exactly the same shape and mode of formation as their sandy counterparts. The far smaller snow barchans* were of the order of ten yards long, and half as wide and up to perhaps eighteen inches high. Just like their sandy relations these snow dunes moved by being blown by the wind. A whole set of barchans formed only a few tens of metres away from our tents.

Watching the evening sky with the sun low in the south was a moving experience. Yet I found that my choice of music in those circumstances was not what I expected it to be. Previously I would have selected something fairly light. Instead I found that I preferred no music to the wrong music. It was almost as if the silence was sacred and was not to be disturbed by man's endeavours. In England, even in the remotest spot, there would be the sounds of birds or insects or the wind in the trees, but on George VI Ice Shelf there was absolutely no sound at all. At one point I found the silence so unsettling that I had to shout so as to make sure that I had not gone deaf. The sound of the wind high in the peaks of the nearby mountains was a comfort when we were not disturbed by the wind directly. All too often though the wind raced off the high plateau of the Antarctic Peninsula down the glaciers as a katabatic wind* gaining speed as it descended. By the time it reached our tent the wind was like a locomotive steaming its way westwards. On one occasion I was standing on a manfood box admiring the scenery when I heard the sound of a new katabatic wind approaching. Within seconds I was hit by gale force winds which struck the tent with a whack then sped on. The wind strength stayed at gale force for thirty six hours and then, as quickly as it had started, it stopped, leaving only a whisper of a breeze in its wake. Only the trail of devastation across the camp told of its recent passage.

On one calm sunny evening, Peter and I decided to spend some time outside taking photographs. Peter took each 'doo for a brief spin, racing as fast as he could along the line of bamboo canes. He tried charging up over a barchan dune which launched him and his 'doo into the air. Such 'doo-jumping practice was not mechanically to be recommended. After his Eval Kenevil stunts Peter retired to the living tent while I continued taking pictures. Before long I too retired to the relative warmth of our tent. Soon afterwards, Peter decided he needed to go outside for a brief moment but could not be bothered to put on his boots. So he crawled out of the tent then tiptoed around the snow valence over the various boxes. Suddenly I heard a yell followed by a loud crash. I poked my head out to see what all the commotion was about. There lay Peter spread-eagled over two sets of guy ropes, laughing his head off.

With continuous daylight for most of the season we found that our daily cycle lengthened to about twenty eight hours per 'day'. This had come about as a result of working both in daytime and overnight. The disadvantage with this was that we had to apply quite a rigid discipline of time keeping in order to keep track of the day of the week. If our timing had become totally dislocated, trying to patch into radio scheds would have become next to impossible. We forced ourselves to keep to the twenty four hour cycle once we realised what our bodies were trying to do. As the season progressed, the sun set lower in the southern sky and eventually dipped below the horizon at night, so making it easier to maintain a truly daily routine. There were times though when I found myself having vivid dreams whilst asleep at night only to have a daytime dream sequel. Once, whilst my thoughts were far from my work I was convinced I could smell a true English Sunday dinner of roast beef and Yorkshire pudding, roast and boiled potatoes, fresh garden peas with a sprig of mint and succulent young carrots with a knob of butter served with thick steaming gravy. The illusion was so real my mouth was watering at the thought of it all; worse than that, the realism was so great I had to go and look around the camp to make me realise that, sadly, it was only a dream.

As my electrical experiments at our present locality were drawing to a close, I had to obtain some cores of ice from a site several miles away. These ice cores would then be returned to Cambridge where I could study them in my laboratory with special equipment (and in more hospitable conditions). The day we decided to go there was low cloud and poor visibility but it was still reasonable for our journey. We set off with our 'doos and one sledge with emergency gear and our drilling equipment. We were at our destination within the hour and set to work. Before long it was snowing hard and visibility had reduced to zero. We were working in a whiteout where sky and ground merged into one indistinguishable blanket. We carried on drilling until lunch time which we spent inside a small pup tent*. We were looking forward to having a nice hot cup of tea from our thermos flask but were disappointed to find the tea stone cold. We ate meat bar raw, gnawing off chunks and chewing the dry concentrate. We also attempted to eat a couple of oranges but these were frozen solid. There were ice crystals inside the orange. After our break from the weather and from drilling we resumed work and managed to complete our task by late afternoon. The new ice cores had been put in polythene tubes and sealed and finally encased in cardboard tubes for transportation. Weather conditions for our return journey were extremely poor. Our tracks from our outward journey had been completely obscured by fresh snow so we had no hope of back tracking. We were forced to navigate solely on compass bearings and dead-reckoning using our sledge wheel. We saw none of the stakes that we had passed on our way over in the morning. We later worked out that we had passed by some stakes by only a few metres. Once we had travelled eight or so miles we turned onto a new compass bearing which should have taken us straight to our main camp. We motored for a mile or so in the zero visibility. We could not see anything. We should have been at our camp but there was no sign of it. Somewhere out there in the whiteness was 'home', but where? I felt cold, really cold. My beard and moustache had both frozen solid. Every time I moved my jaw I could feel the ice around my mouth crack and pull on the hairs of my beard. My nose felt as if it had frost nip but I could not tell. I had no sense of feeling in my hands or my face. We decided that the safest course of action was to pitch the pup tent and wait until visibility improved sufficiently for us to either see our camp or to spot some landmark from which we could take a new bearing. We were in no immediate danger; we had food, a stove and fuel. The question was just how long would we have to stay in what was a very small tent in very cramped conditions? Even inside the single-skinned tent the temperature was well below zero and our breath condensed in front of us and froze around our mouths and noses. We drank some soup and two more meat bars. The best place for us then was in our sleeping bags. It was the only way to try to preserve any heat that we had. We clambered into our sleeping bags fully dressed. Our predicament had meant that we were separated from our radio which was still in base camp. The time had slipped by and we had missed our evening radio sched. Rothera would wonder where we were. Before long I had dozed off, quite content to stay in my warm pit* until next morning for a break in the weather. Two hours later Peter woke me up. He had had a look outside and the mank had lifted. He had seen a flag from which he had deduced our exact position. We struck camp quickly hoping to reach our main camp before the weather closed in again. The tent was down and packed up in no time, but our problems were not over. Peter's 'doo would not start. The carburettor had frozen up which meant he had to dismantle it and clean it with methylated spirit. All this made him furious and he became extremely touchy. Any slight error of judgement or mistimed question on my part sent him into a tantrum. The clouds had now lifted sufficiently to let the sun be seen. Its light caught the edges of the clouds and tinged them with silver. The newly fallen powder snow had a reddish hue from the low angle of the setting sun. The adjacent mountains on Alexander Island were robed in a haze of pink. By midnight we were ready. Peter's 'doo was fixed and idling well although Peter was still rather boot*. Peter shot off on his 'doo in a cloud of powder snow as he raced towards our main camp. I had to travel somewhat slower as my 'doo had to haul the sledge with all my valuable ice cores. I tried to follow in Peter's tracks but contrast* was still poor and on occasions I ploughed through deep soft snow sending up a fine white spray all around. Then I saw our tents with their bright orange flanks highlighted by a sparkle of sunlight. It was good to have returned. Feeling somewhat relieved I unloaded the ice cores into our pit. Where we had stopped over in the pup tent must have been only half a mile from our main camp and we had passed by the far end of my cable array with all its flags and canes literally by only a few yards. We eventually finished our chores by 1 o'clock in the morning. Peter lit the primus for a brew and also the Tilley lamp for heat and light. It was the first time in the season that we had really needed the lamp for light. With a cup of hot steaming sweet cocoa Peter calmed down and became more sociable. I felt exhausted and fell asleep very quickly.

Outside the clouds had descended once more and snow began falling, blown by a strengthening wind.

The weather stayed bad for the next thirty six hours or so; the gusting wind whipped up the powder snow in ground drift which whisped over the frozen surface. Peter and I spent the morning repairing damaged kit and torn clothing, and as most of my electrical experimentation was completed, it was time to dismantle the array. The remainder of the day was spent on minor chores and, after dinner Peter and I swapped medical anecdotes. I recounted the case of my medical examination prior to going south. I was sitting in the doctor's waiting room when a lady in a white tunic beckoned to me to go through to the surgery. I turned to the woman and, as I knew I was to have a full medical, said 'Shall I take my clothes off now?' She replied with a wry grin on her face 'You can if you like but I'm just the receptionist!' My jaw dropped and my face blushed as I realised my mistake. A moment or two later, another white-coated woman came into the room, grinning broadly 'You can take your clothes off now!' she said, 'I am the doctor.'

Our radio sched that evening was uneventful. We heard that HMS *Endurance* had reached Rothera along with a large pile of mail. The thought of more letters cheered us up. We informed Rothera that if we were to move to our next destination we were going to need some more 'doo fuel as we were running short. To us that was a minor inconvenience as if there was any trouble we could always be flown out. Then Flo' informed us that one plane was grounded and the other plane had gone to Punta Arenas to pick up a spare part. Our fuel shortage took on a new light. We would be lucky if our fuel lasted us to Fossil Bluff. Unless we had more fuel we were in a bit of a predicament. After the sched during which we were told to stay put for the time, Peter and I tried to assess our situation carefully and plan alternative strategies for an overland evacuation. We had great thoughts of us having to sledge up onto the plateau as far north as Rothera, then west as far as we could to the coast and await a pick up by one of the ships, if one could break through the ice. Such thoughts were distinctly uncomfortable and I prayed hard that such an epic journey would be unnecessary. If we just hung around waiting for ever, I would never finish my season's work. I had a battle with myself to try to reason which pieces of kit, specimens, etc, could be depoted* without jeopardising my research later in Cambridge. At the same time I was trying to think positively about our own safety. However, I was loath to leave anything scientific behind if I could possibly help it. We were told to come up on the radio sched at 0800 hours next morning for an update.

Sleep that night came fitfully interspersed with dreams about possible eventualities – the long sledge journey with all its many dangers, or starving to death in the middle of the sound; each scenario being exaggerated to ridiculous limits by an over-vivid imagination. After what had seemed an interminable time, morning arrived. We picked up Rothera on the radio as arranged. 'One plane en route Marambio with spare part, other one should be flyable later today. If all OK, you'll have your resupply tomorrow.' Relief! I knew those dreams were ridiculous! If a plane was due in that meant I could write Sue another letter and it would be posted long before I returned to base. Peter and I both set about our writing pads in a frenzy. Peter's pen gave up the ghost half way through a particularly passionate paragraph. He lit the primus to heat up his pen to revitalise the flow of ink. Suddenly there was a pop and Peter sat holding a pen whose ink cartridge had ruptured. Ink was splattered all over him and his letter was now covered in thick blotches of ink and looked like a Dalmatian's coat.

Next morning we awoke to a dingle day which was very flyable as far as we could see. We radioed Rothera and gave our met. obs. We were asked to come back at two hourly intervals. Peter manned the radio at 10 and 12 o'clock. At the latter sched, we were given only ten minutes' notice that Alpha Quebec* was en route to us from Gomez Nunatak having dumped off some kit there. Sure enough, the telltale drone of an aircraft's engine could be heard. We scanned the sky and spotted the plane, tiny against the backdrop of the icefall of Goodenough Glacier. Moments later it swooped down over the camp, circled and landed. We felt invaded as there were five people on board and everyone wanted a cup of tea. It was great to see new faces and to laugh and chat with someone different for a brief while. One of the pilots was a real mischief maker and within moments everyone was involved in a massive snowball fight. At the 1 pm radio sched we were told that the other Twotter, Alpha Whiskey*, would also be calling in as Fossil Bluff was fog bound. We renamed ourselves 'Oscar International Airport'. With one Twotter already on the ground we had to give clear instructions to Alpha Whiskey's pilot so he knew in which direction to approach. The second plane was with us before we really knew what was happening. On board her were another six people which brought Sledge Oscar's compliment to thirteen. This was definitely a case of overcrowding. However, there were now sufficient people to make up a game of cricket. One spade stuck into the snow made one wicket and another spade served as the cricket bat. A soft ball magically appeared and the game was under way. The wicket left a lot to be desired but we all had a great time. There was also a serious task to be done in that one plane needed to be refuelled before continuing on its journey. One plane had to be carefully taxied close to the other so that fuel could be transferred. It was quite an amazing sight to behold – two red and black Twin Otter aircraft wing tip to wing tip and thirteen men running around with a spade and a fluorescent pink ball all stuck in the middle of an apparently featureless ice shelf. During the stay of the two planes a couple of scientists on board spent time with me chatting about our respective research. It was a real breath of fresh air to be able to talk to people with a kindred spirit on the scientific side. Eventually, both planes departed, one to Fossil Bluff, and the other one in the opposite direction to '82 Bravo'*. With the planes gone the camp seemed emptier than before. It was as if the presence of those extra faces had suddenly brought home to me that there were only the two of us there miles from anywhere. We had given our letters to Barry and they were bound for Rothera. We had taken delivery of a forty-five-gallon drum of 'doo fuel which would be quite sufficient for our purposes. We could finish off our work at that site and think seriously about a move to our next, and last, site.

That evening I thought back over the season so far and what I have achieved. I had books full of numbers and observations, boxes full of samples and a head full of ideas. I had plenty on which to work once back in Cambridge. Even if I achieved nothing more over the following weeks before being recalled to base, I knew I had had a good field season. Anything else would be a bonus. My thoughts turned to the letter I had written to Sue and I seriously wondered whether I had overstepped the mark in what I had said to her. I hoped I had not jeopardised our relationship by saying anything foolish. If only I had had a long letter from her to tell me what she was feeling about me. If only, if only! That seemed to be my catchphrase. My concern about my relationship with Sue seemed to have subsided somewhat over the weeks that I had been in the field now that I was more engrossed in my work. I had absolutely no control over what was happening between Sue and myself because of the lack of communication. I would have to be patient. It was as though I was becoming reconciled to our separation and coming to terms with it. What was more pressing to me at that stage was the journey that lay ahead over the next few days. One advantage of static camps was that one could really settled down and make it a bit homely, but a mobile camp at a new site each

Top: Hope Bay – my first sight of Antarctica.
Bottom: An iceberg drifts slowly by in Drake Passage.

Top: A clear trail is cut through sea ice by RRS Bransfield south of the Lemaire Channel.
Bottom left: A sleepy seal basks at Damoy.
Bottom right: A husky at Rothera.

Top: A night-time football game on sea ice with RRS Bransfield being used as a goal.
Bottom: Faraday base.

Top: A 2-am pause whilst sledging on George VI Ice Shelf.
Centre: A Twin Otter brings welcome post and supplies to our field camp.
Bottom: Impromptu skidoo repairs some 60 miles south of the elusive Eternity Range.

Top: Field camp on the Goodenough Glacier, George VI Ice Shelf.
Bottom: The camp becomes engulfed by drifting snow.

Top: Frozen seascape near Rothera.
Bottom: Rothera base, Adelaide Island. The two-storey building (*centre*) is the main accommodation block with the 'potting shed' nearby (*left*).

Top: Nesting penguins at Damoy.
Bottom: Stanley Cathedral, Falkland Islands, with its whalebone arch.

Top: The historic Lutheran church at Grytviken, South Georgia.
Bottom: The vestments (*left*) of the last incumbent adorn the front of the small church at Grytviken. The altar verse (in Norwegian) is Matthew 11, verse 28.

night was more like basic survival. In one sense, I was looking ahead to the new adventure with all its new challenges. In another, I was dreading it for all its uncertainties and dangers. Yet the presence of those very dangers provided a real excitement and, if we survived the journey, there would be the satisfaction of having won through against adversity. With all these thoughts buzzing around in my mind I set to my tasks of tidying up and packing ready for the off the following day. My work on Georve VI Ice Shelf was over for this year.

7: Towards Eternity

After a hearty breakfast Peter and I struck camp and packed up the sledges. The weather was poor – hardly an auspicious start to our 200-mile journey to Mount Charity high on the plateau of the Antarctic Peninsula. We had to brush the snow off the sledges even as we lashed them up. I managed to gash my hand whilst roping up some boxes, having caught a finger against one of the hooks on the side of the sledge. I applied a dressing but the bleeding was quite persistent. I redressed the wound and put my gloves back on. We had to get a move on.

To look over our now deserted camp site was quite a strange sensation. All that remained as evidence of our stay was a flat area where the tent had been pitched, and a snowdrift on what had been the windward side of the tent. The ground was littered with out footprints and extending out in two long straight lines were our tracks which marked out where the arrays had been. Within a day, all these marks would be covered over and there would be no trace of our having been there at all.

Peter attached the rope to his sledge from his 'doo and signalled that he was ready. I was all set on my 'doo; hopefully everything was securely tied on. If anything fell off Peter's sledge or 'doo I would be able to spot it, but there was no one behind me to pick up my pieces.

The silence was shattered as two 'doos sparked into life. Within minutes we were off. Periodically I had to glance backwards over my sledge to make sure everything was all right. I rode side saddle to make it easier to get on and off my 'doo and also to check on the sledge behind. The caterpillar tracks at the back sent up clouds of snow spray as we powered our way northwards. The Nansen sledges glided smoothly over the soft snow surface. All that we left behind us was our tracks.

About eleven miles north of our last camp we encountered masses of frozen over melt-pools. The lake ice was turquoise blue and was hard as concrete. Some of the ice was fractured by the movement of the ice shelf and had formed small ridges about three feet high. We circumnavigated these without difficulty. The further north we went the more extensive the areas of lake ice became. We had to go carefully over the lake ice because if we over-revved, the caterpillar tracks lost traction which could set the 'doo into a spin. This happened to me once. Peter had crossed one lake without too much trouble and I tried to follow. His 'doo had effectively cleaned the ice surface of any soft snow on which my vehicle's tracks could bite. The next thing I knew was my 'doo was slowly spinning through 360 degrees and my sledge had overtaken me. When I tried very carefully to apply some throttle, the tracks just spun round and round and I went nowhere. It was like sitting on top of a large floor polisher. In time I managed to extricate myself from this ridiculous position while Peter just sat on his 'doo watching me, laughing.

After a couple more hours, we reached the foot of Armstrong Glacier. Our route meant we had to ascend this glacier to gain access to the top of the plateau of the Antarctic Peninsula. This part of our journey was to take us from near sea level to 2,500 feet via the Batterbee Mountains. However, our way up the glacier was barred by a melt-water stream flowing south. Further north the stream broadened considerably into a braided section. We turned our vehicles and drove parallel with the stream to find a way across it. For the sake of safety while traversing crevasse fields on the glacier, we roped up. I was attached to a rope tied to the back karabina* of the 'doo, and also by a short cord to an emergency stop button on the 'doo's dash panel. I was also wearing a Whillan's sit harness to which my ropes were attached. Suspended from this harness were two jumars* by which, should I have had the misfortune to fall down a crevasse and still be uninjured, I could climb up the rope and out to safety. My 'doo was connected to the back of Peter's sledge by another rope and he was harnessed to his 'doo in a similar manner to me. The roping configuration we had used meant that if either of us went down into a crevasse, the 'doo engine would stop (the emergency stop button having been activated), and the vehicle would dangle by the rope which connected it either to a sledge or to the other 'doo which would act as a brake. Fortunately all these precautions proved unnecessary although they were of considerable comfort. We were travelling in a known crevasse field and most of the crevasses were very obvious and hence easy to avoid. There were others, however, which were concealed beneath snow bridges. The larger ones could be spotted as the snow bridges tended to sag and we knew not to even attempt crossing. Once, I was following Peter over some smooth ground when I heard a low whoomph and felt my skidoo lurch. The snow immediately beneath me collapsed into a deep crevasse. For one long moment I watched as the snow bridge disappeared into a gaping dark blue abyss. Thankfully, the crevasse was only about three feet wide and the bridge had given way just as the front end of the caterpillar tracks had reached the far side of the crevasse but it was unnerving to say the least.

I found it difficult driving as I had to watch the rope ahead of me so that it would not catch under the front ski of my 'doo. I also had to try to match my speed with that of the sledge in front of me. If I went too fast, I ran over the linking rope; if too slow, I put extra strain onto Peter's 'doo. I knelt on the 'doo seat to gain that extra bit of height for better visibility and to give more control of the handlebars over rough terrain.

Once I caught the linking rope by mistake and it wrapped itself around my 'doo's front ski. We had to stop to unravel it which did not please Peter very much. He flew off the handle at me and told me to maintain constant speed. We stood next to the front of my 'doo and looked at the rope. We thought the ground sounded different when we stepped on it so Peter took the bog chisel from my 'doo and thrust it into the snow. It went straight through. He tried elsewhere in front of him with the same effect. He tried to the side, the same; then behind and still the same. We were standing on a large snow bridge over what must have been a very large crevasse. The consequences did not bear thinking about if that bridge had collapsed then. We gingerly sorted out the tangled rope then inched our way off the bridge. I was very relieved once onto firmer ice.

At the upper part of the glacier the going was easier so we stopped where it was safe to check the 'doo over. It provided a breathing space to be able to look at the scenery. The weather had improved considerably. We could see Mount Bagshawe quite plainly, its austere stark form towered some 7,000 feet above us. The reds and pinks of the granite cut through black rock adjacent to it. Looking back down the glacier we could see the clouds in George VI Sound, grey and thick to the west of us. We had reached about 3,000 feet above sea level and the air temperature was correspondingly lower. The sun was bright and the radiation fierce. I plastered my face with sun-filter cream to avoid being sunburnt and more lipsalve to try to ease my sore, cracked lips.

The next part of our route was to veer north-east which was to take us from the upper reaches of Armstrong Glacier to the lower flanks of the plateau ice sheet. As we reached the higher ground, so more and more of the scenery came into view. We could see right over to the LeMay Range in the centre of Alexander Island, some seventy five miles distant. To the east, the ice rose still higher.

The ice over which we were to travel was considered to be free of crevasses and so we untied our connecting rope from Peter's sledge to my 'doo. We reached a flat level area to the east of the Batterbee Mountains, roughly east of Fossil Bluff. We raced onwards for a while until the lateness of the day and physical fatigue suggested that it was time to pitch camp if we could find some shelter. We drove until we had reached Mount Cadbury whose peak rose to just under 5,000 feet. Huge contorted lobes of ice hung precariously on the mountain's flanks, the blue-white ice broken by crevasses and avalanche tracks. The 2,000 feet of nunatak which comprised Mount Cadbury was the only immediate feature other than a vast expanse of desolate looking ice. It lacked the beauty which other icescapes had had and I thought it was quite horrible. After covering fifty four miles in seven hours we stopped for the night. Within a few minutes, the tent was up and Peter disappeared through the tunnel entrance and started sorting everything out and put a brew on. By half past seven I was glad to have finished for the day and to be able to relax in comparative comfort and warmth.

I slept very badly despite being so tired and woke around four in the morning. My sleeping bag was covered in rime frost as were the inside walls of the tent. It was my turn to cook breakfast, during which I managed to knock over a billy of water. The groundsheet was awash, but very quickly the water froze and so did everything that had been wetted. Peter was furious and really let me have an earful. Fortunately no real damage was done.

The weather was ideal for travelling with brilliant sunshine in an almost cloudless sky. We were soon packed up and ready to leave on the next stage of our journey. Within minutes we encountered sastrugi, ridges of wind-blown snow which have compacted as hart as concrete and whose intricate forms had been sculpted by strong driving winds. These features reduced our travelling speed to a fast walking pace. We had to weave our wy around these ridges as to have crossed over them directly would have damaged our 'doos or laden sledges. We were heading north-north-east and were slowly climbing higher onto the ice sheet. After covering twenty one miles in three hours we stopped for lunch. We pitched the pup tent between the two sledges to provide us with respite from the bitterly cold wind and, once inside, ate our chocolate ration with a cup of luke warm tea. Our thermos flask had been damaged and was no longer a good insulator. My beard and moustache had iced up solid around my mouth from frozen condensed breath. We both decided to put on our padded sledging trousers beneath our windproofs. It made us look like astronauts and movement was cumbersome but at least we felt warm again. I also put on an extra inner glove on my right hand which had tended to become very cold from holding the throttle. My original inner glove was caked in congealed blood from my gashed finger but at least the wound had dried somewhat and felt more comfortable.

To the east of where we had stopped we could make out the summit of Mount Andrew Jackson, the highest peak in the whole Antarctic Peninsula at 14,500 feet.

After our lunch break we relashed the sledges and continued on our way north-north-east. The sastrugi were even bigger than before, reaching heights of two feet or more. I noticed that there were also some barchan dunes. The various snow structures slowed our rate of progress down even more. We had to zigzag around the sastrugi watching our sledges carefully as they slid at alarming angles over the snow ridges. It was a tremendous testimony to the good design and sturdy construction of those Nansen sledges that with over 1,000 pounds of weight on them, the wooden frames twisted, bent and distorted to an amazing degree and yet nothing broke. Polar expeditions which had tried all-metal sledges soon found that they disintegrated under such treatment and the wood and leather Nansens were brought out to replace their alloy would-be usurpers.

However, the sastrugi took their toll during the afternoon: one of my 'doo's wheel axles had flipped upside down and the caterpillar track was loose. Peter had two wheel axles in a similar state. In addition, one of his had lost a nut and the other had been bent skew. We stopped to consider our position. We could see the northern part of Alexander Island about 150 miles away to the north-west in its scenic splendour. In front of us to the north east was barren sterile plateau stretching as far as we could see. We repaired our wheel axles and started off again. At the same time, the wind strengthened and began to cause ground drift. As we drove on we climbed still higher and the temperature dropped even lower. Visibility decreased as the ground drift picked up. The wind swirled the dry snow around violently. Squalls of powder snow vortexed at us with a vengeance. Yet high above us the sun was as bright as ever. As the ground drift worsened, my beard froze up even more chilling my face. Even with my padded overtrousers on I still feld cold. Soon conditions for travelling were very poor; the ground drift was at least seven feet deep so shrouding us in next to zero visibility. I had to follow Peter quite closely for fear of losing sight of him. Peter decided enough was enough and so we stopped to pitch camp and sit out the storm. I was glad to have a chance to be out of that bitingly cold wind. My face thawed out and flushed from the rejuvination of the blood circulation. It was like a small portion of heaven to feel warm again and to have some hot food inside. I managed to upset another billy of water inside the tent. I expected a tirade from Peter but to my amazement, he just joked about it. We managed to make contact with Rothera on the evening sched so we passed on our latest QTH. We were able to have a quick witter with Sledge Hotel who were already at the depot near Mount Charity and to which we were valiantly plying our way. As we sat listening to the radio the tent gradually frosted up. A white icy line started at ground level then worked its way slowly up the inside walls of the tent to about head height. Once the primus and the Tilley lamp were extinguished, the temperature in the tent plummeted even further.

Despite the noise of the wind, we both managed to sleep well. When we awoke the inside of the tent was completely rimed up. It was like waking up inside a deep freeze. The water in one of the billies was frozen into a solid lump as had our reconstituted milk. We stayed in our pits to keep warm whilst we made breakfast. We were able to portion out our milk very easily even though it was frozen. We just dunked the solid block into our tea and melted off the required amount.

The wind continued unabated until late afternoon when there was a lull. We dug out the 'doos where the snow had drifted all over them and prepared them for travel. By early evening, the wind was buffetting the tent once more. We decided against travelling and prepared for another night in our temporary camp. That evening we tried to raise Rothera on the radio but comms were so bad we could not either hear anyone else or be heard. We were totally cut off from the outside world and the storm was worsening.

Next morning there was yet more wind and snow pounding against the tent. We stayed put until late morning. The weather then looked as fair as it was going to be and so we decided to go. From initial lethargy early that morning, Sledge Oscar was transformed into frantic activity. The sledges were prepared, the 'doos cleaned down, the tent dug out and the sledges packed and lashed up. We fired up the 'doos and set off northwards still ascending. The wind and ground drift was unpleasant but we could manage it. The air temperature was around $-17°C$ although the wind chill factor made it feel as if it were $-55°C$. My beard and moustache again froze quickly.

We continued for another couple of miles until the conditions became impossible. I was having trouble seeing Peter up front and even my sledge kept disappearing behind a white misty veil. The whiteout conditions created a very weird sensation. I became completely disorientated. At one stage I thought, incorrectly, that we were sledging south instead of north and that we were going down an incline when we should have been on the flat. Fortunately the sun was just visible at times through the cloud and snow so I was able to re-establish my sense of direction by that. At one stage we even steered by the wind. We knew its direction so we kept at a constant angle to it, making sure that the wind had not veered by watching where we were with respect to the sun, when possible, and relative to the direction of sastrugi which reflected that of the prevailing wind. The cold was unbearable. Peter circled round and signalled to stop. There was no point trying to speak as the din of the wind drowned out any attempt at speech. We had the tent up in a matter of only ten minutes but in that short time I experienced the worst physical conditions I have ever encountered. My goggles froze over with the powder snow so I removed them to be able to see what I was doing with the tent. My ordinary glasses soon became likewise fogged but when I came to wipe the snow off them, my finger stuck to the frames. My glasses had frozen onto my face, and my eyelashes were beginning to freeze together so that each blink of an eyelid was more difficult as my eyes started to freeze shut. My beard and moustache were completely caked in ice and I had icicles three inches long hanging from my chin. I could not move my lower jaw for the ice and the deep cold. To be able to climb into the tent out of that wind was like stepping in front of a warm fire. Peter and I both sat in the tent with a billy each held under our chins to collect the water as the ice in our beards slowly melted with the warmth of the stove. To try to pull the ice from one's beard was an act of masochism. To melt it out was by far the less painful if more time consuming method.

We had been sledging for four days, one and a half days more than the whole journey should have taken and we were still tens of miles from our destination. The atrocious conditions had made the journey into a nightmare. The only respite was the relative comfort and warmth of the tent and how precarious that had been at times. It made me realise how fragile was the line that marked survival from disaster. I was relieved that we were still on the winning side. The remainder of the day was spent sitting out the storm with plenty of time to think of the situation we were in and of the events that had befallen us. Since leaving our last camp site on George VI Ice Shelf I had had the assurance from the Lord that we would reach our destination, but it had meant a great deal of prayer en route, prayer for safe keeping and a prayer of thankfulness after that escape from the collapsing snow bridge and from the fearsome storms. All through the morning I had been praying that the wind would subside but the opposite happened. It made me wonder what use was prayer when it did not appear to work. I recalled the story of Job, of how he had suffered but won through with patience, faith and a real trust in God. So I rethought my position and thanked the Lord for such dreadful conditions and that we had both been kept safe so far. Our last few hours prior to stopping that morning had a spiritual message to them. Our physical disorientation was a result of not having any landmarks by which to fix our position. Was not that true of us spiritually? The common search for one's spirituality sent many a person off on strange journeys, geographical as well as spiritual. We would search in vain trying to find the way ahead and all too frequently arriving back where we had already been. We were spiritually disorientated. When we spotted the sun shining even though so weakly through those swirling snow filled clouds, we had found something by which to navigate. So too if we were to look to the Son of God, we would also find direction to our lives, and a sense of assurance as I had had that morning, of knowing that despite feelings to the contrary when the sun was not visible, that we were going in the right way. If only more people could have realised that their searching would end if only they took time or made the effort to find the Son. As John 14, verse 6 clearly states: 'Jesus answered him [the disciple Thomas], "I am the way, the truth and the life; no one goes to the Father except by me" '. In addition, just as Peter and I frequently lost sight of the sun, it did not mean that the sun was not there, it was only that we could not see it from where we were at the time. I felt that far too many people thought that of Christ, that as they could not sense him all of the time, he was not there. Far from it, I knew that his very existence surrounded us and that he was constantly with us. No storm could have removed him from us or us from him. I knew then with a real reassurance that we would reach our destination safely. That was not to say it would all be plain sailing or that we would not feel the cold, but just that we would get there whole.

The next morning Peter and I awoke almost simultaneously and both of us with a start. It was not noise which had woken us but silence. We poked our heads out of the tent and we were greeted by the most perfect morning we could have wanted. Clear blue cloudless sky and a flat calm, not even a hint of a breeze. Visibility was excellent. We could make out Mount Charity away on the horizon to the north, some sixty miles away. Contrast was good too so we would actually be able to see what we were travelling over. We quickly packed up our camp not wanting to waste the good weather. The storm had left miles and miles of large sastrugi which we battled our way through. The sledges suffered a real hammering as did the 'doos. One bogey wheel on my 'doo kept on flipping over. Just before midday, three axles broke simultaneously on one side of Peter's 'doo which looked a very sorry, and rather lopsided sight. We had successfully travelled over twenty one miles. We would not be able to do one mile more unless we could repair Peter's 'doo. We were very thankful for the good weather as it made Peter's job that much easier without having to contend with blowing snow whilst trying to furkle* with bolts and spanners. After an hour and a half and much swearing and cursing from Peter, our vehicles were patched up. Peter was able to replace one of the broken bogies with a spare, but the other two could not be replaced. Instead, he took one bogey from my 'doo and put it on his so we each were one bogey down. If we were fortunate that would suffice until we reached Mount Charity. We drove on towards the Eternity range which consisted of three main peaks named mounts Faith, Hope and Charity; and the greatest of those was Hope, not Charity as might have been expected. How the 'Eternity' range had been named was reputed to be that no matter from which direction the mountains were approached, it took an eternity to reach them. As far as we were concerned, there was more truth in that than was comfortable.

Within minutes of setting off again, we lost sight of Mount Charity because of the topography of the plateau. Two hours later we reached the top of a prominent rise and Mount Charity loomed up at us far larger than when we had last seen it. We could see that the sastrugi died out to the north. Several times during those two hours we had to stop to weaken the fuel/oil mixture on the carburettors because of the change in altitude; we were then at over 6,000 feet above sea level. On one such stop, Peter's 'doo refused to start. It had a faulty magneto and he was able to do only a bodge job on it. It would only have been problematical if we had to keep on stopping so we resolved to keep going until we reached our destination, if at all possible. It was not. First of all we had to refuel. Then Peter's P-bag* fell off from the back of his 'doo, and lastly his sledge wheel came off. In this last case, Peter had not realised that he had lost something so I stopped to pick up the wheel while he blazed on ahead. I nursed the wheel on my lap while sitting side saddle for the next twenty minutes until I caught up with Peter. I was relieved to relinquish the wheel. My arm was stiff from holding it in the cold for so long.

At our last repair stop, we noticed that a heavy bank of mank was approaching the plateau from the north-west. It was going to be a real race against time and the elements if we were to reach Mount Charity before being engulfed in yet more bad weather. Soon we reached flat ground where, thankfully, the sastrugi died right out. Our rate of progress increased markedly and we stormed on northwards as fast as our sickening 'doos would take us.

As we neared our objective so the low cloud moved closer and closer. Before long we were engulfed in swirling clouds. Contrast vanished and everything looked a shade of grey. I began to despair of not actually arriving at our derstination. I was so tired of travellng, yet I knew in my inner man that we would make it. Both Peter and I thought we only had five miles to go, but in reality it was eighteen. On we went. At times we were in a whiteout and I hoped and prayed that we were going in a straight line. It was all too easy to veer off without realising it. The tension was killing. The conditions were worsening by the minute. We had to get there quickly. Suddenly, Peter pointed to his right and changed course. He had seen the nunatek which was to be our home until the end of the season. We were some eight miles distant. The small nunatak kept on disappearing from view as the white swirling mass wrapped itself around us. Moments later I saw two bright orange objects at the foot of the nunatak – Sledge Hotel's tents. We raced on even harder, willing our 'doos to find that extra power to speed us there all the faster. At least the ground was free of sastrugi. The distance between the tents and ourselves seemed to stay forever far. Gradually I could discern the tents clearly, some flagged poles and then two people standing by the tents. They had heard us. We were going to make it! We rolled into the camp area at 7.10 pm shattered but over the moon at having arrived. Praise the Lord! We were warmly greeted by Julian and his GA, Tim, both of whom had been at the depot site all season. We had completed sixty five miles despite all the mechanical problems. We just left the 'doos and sledges fully laden and climbed into Sledge Hotel's living tent. Tim had prepared us a brew and most welcome it was too. Peter and I pitched out tent a little distant from that of Hotel and unloaded the gear we needed straight away. The remaining kit we lashed onto the sledges and prepared our camp in case of storm. Although the wind was blowing and the cloud base was down to the ground, it had not deteriorated as we thought it might. We all crammed into Hotel's dining tent which was renamed on our arrival the 'Hotel Annex'. Tim very kindly cooked evening scradge for all four of us. We all felt better for having that inside us. Julian did the evening sched on our behalf. The absence of communications from us for three nights had caused considerable concern at Rothera. When the news of our safe arrival was announced there was great relief, and in the radio shack, clapping that we had made it. For the rest of the evening, the four of us chatted away excitedly and all the previous tensions vanished. I had to keep on pinching myself to make me believe that we were truly at 'Mount Charity Depot'. As I lay in my pit trying to sleep, I could not help but feel elated as well as exhausted. On reflection, it felt good to have been through all that we had endured. I felt I had really experienced Antarctica in one of her harsher moods and we had come through safely. Thank God!

8: Faith, Hope and Charity

The morning after our arrival at Mount Charity Depot was beautiful. It was very cold though, around −20°C. I could see Mount Charity very clearly standing proud eight miles north of us. A wisp of cloud sat aloft the main peak like a small furry cap. Peter repaired his skidoo while I sorted out my boxes of scientific equipment. There was no sound from Sledge Hotel, they were obviously still fast asleep in their pits. Once my kit was in order, I explored the few rock exposures on the nunatak where I found plenty to interest me: a type of granite and its margin and fascinating associated mineralization. I took several pieces for my collection at home. Around 10.30 am, Julian emerged, bleary eyed, from his living tent. We found that Sledge Hotel's day started around three hours later than ours, and finished correspondingly later. Julian and I pitched my work tent over one of the boreholes that he and Tim had drilled during the season. When we had finished, we went on a guided tour of the nunatak. We climbed to the top of the nunatak from which we had a superb panoramic view of the Eternity Range. To descend we slid down a long snowbank to the camp, a very fast and fun way of doing it. Julian then took us to the ice cave that they had excavated during the season. The nunatak was flanked by drapes of old hard ice, some of which was crevassed. It was into this ice that Sledge Hotel had dug in order to provide short-term cold storage for several hundred yards of ice core tubes. This facility was to provide space for important ice samples which were to be drilled later during a deep borehole project. As the Twotters were only able to carry a limited number of core boxes at a time, the remaining ice core boxes needed to be kept as cold as possible and out of the warming rays of the sun. This cave provided the ideal solution. Inside the temperature was even colder than outside and the chill of the air took one's breath away. At the back of the cave through a small passage we were shown a natural cavity which had formed between the ice and the rock of the nanatak. Hanging from the ceiling and from the walls were some of the most exquisite ice crystals I had ever seen. They were perfect in every detail and enormous too. Feathers of delicate ice hung into the void and were ten or more inches long. Clusters of crystals took on the appearance of cut glass rose blooms as large as one's fist. Yet it was nigh on impossible to pluck one of these ice flowers without it disintegrating into a tinkle of brittle ice. We took a Tilley lamp inside the cavern so we could take some photographs. Natural light filtered through the ice walls and cast everything in a blue glow. With the white light from the lamp the ice crystals sparkled as if tinted with diamonds. It was a remarkable grotto. Unfortunately, my camera froze up in the intense cold and so I could not record the scene for posterity.

For the remainder of the day Julian and I discussed our research work in one of the tents while Tim and Peter checked over the 'doos and our field kit. There was talk of them attempting to climb down into the large crevasse to the south of the camp to see how far they could go laterally inside it.

The following morning Julian and I worked in the laboratory tent over the hole. We were testing a borehole probe I had built to see if it would detect different layers within the ice beneath us. Peering down the hole I could see the blue glow that is characteristic of sunlight through snow, with the blueness darkening to black as the hole went deeper and deeper. When we took the cover off the hole there was a strong updraught of cold air. We assembled the probe and the various measuring instruments and a bank of batteries. We switched on and lowered the probe, picking up some signals, and were quite pleased but something was still not correct. We upped the voltage to 540 V to see what effect that would have and lowered the probe again. As the device reached the top of the hole after being pulled up again, I touched part of the probe. A surge of electricity shot up my arm and flung me backwards across the tent. I lay dazed not quite knowing what had happened. Julian had quickly disconnected the batteries and came to my aid. The probe had had a short circuit and I had touched part of it which should have been inert. Julian gave me some chocolate as I was still in shock.

The following day, we dispensed with the borehole probe as we had done as much with it as we could. In the afternoon we did some electrical work and laid out our grid which we were going to survey in detail; it was an area of only ten yards long by five wide. We were taking measurements at every eighteen inches over the whole area. When we started the temperature was −16°C but fell to nearly −20° during the course of the afternoon. Such temperatures made writing and fiddling with the knobs on the instruments quite difficult. At first there was no trouble but by the time we were half way through the experiment, it became hard work even to grip a pencil. I had to hold a knob between my index finger and thumb and then step around the electronic box turning the knob as required as I went; all manual dexterity in my hands had gone. The experiment went very well and we had finished in time for the evening sched prior to dinner. There was an air letter from Sue for me. One part of her message puzzled me. The message was 'Many are cold but few are frozen'. Later I realised that this was a new rendering of Matthew 22, verse 14: 'Many are called but few are chosen'. Perhaps there ought to have been a new translation of the Gospels into the AV – Antarctic Version –

of the Bible. We also heard over the sched that we were to be picked up within a day or so. All the other field parties were being recalled as the season was virtually over and it was time to go home. We were not disappointed at the news. We had been out in the field for fifty days of which only three were lie-ups. Poor Sledge Yankee had to lie up 50 per cent of the time. We started to prepare ourselves mentally for being picked up by the planes. Work was effectively over as we had achieved all that we had wanted. We were ready to go back to base. We started to look forward with growing anticipation to the luxury of being back in 'civilisation' as opposed to the rigours of field life. After over seven weeks working each and every day all day and into most evenings, and overnight in some cases, we had done as much in that time as we would have done in almost twice as long back in England. We were all becoming run down and in need of a break, and even more in need of a good wash. We were wearing the same clothes as when we were flown into the field two months before. There was no way of having a shower or a bath. We occasionally tried to have a towel down when we could but it was not the same. Anyway, we did not notice the smell. Our faces were brown and weathered and we looked as if we had been in the field that long. There was also the consideration that the Antarctic winter was drawing closer by the day. The sun was setting below the horizon at night and daytime temperatures were commonly −20°C. With the wind chill factor, we had been working in conditions which felt more like −40 below when outside.

That evening, the preparation of dinner was a team affair and my contribution was to make a favourite dessert of mine, 'veiled peasant girl', a traditional Norwegian recipe which I had acquired when working over there some years before. I overdid the portions and we ended up feeling overfull, and it felt great. Peter and I left Sledge Hotel and I checked the air temperature just before turning in for the night; it was −24°C and falling.

The next couple of days passed by with no plan and with all the work having been finished. The camp had been tidied and the scientific gear packed ready for shipment back to base. The weather where we were remained reasonable. The weather elsewhere in the peninsula, however, was far from amenable and the planes had been grounded. We were asked to come up on the radio at more frequent intervals which tended to add to the frustration of being isolated. At least the four of us got on well with each other.

During the afternoon and evening all four of us convened in the Hotel Annex to while away the time together. Later in the evening we listened to the BBC World Service on a short wave radio which Julian had brought with him. I tuned in to the news for the first time since leaving England and soon realised why I had not missed listening to it over the field season; all the news was bad news. Russia was threatening China who had invaded Vietnam; Teheran was being openly hostile to Israel; strikes back in England and so on. I switched off in disgust – why did Man have to always fight his fellow human beings? How real was the East-West confrontation in human terms as opposed to government policies? I felt sure that if the decisions about Russian isolation from the capitalist West were left to the ordinary men in the streets the iron curtain would be drawn aside in no time at all. What advantage could there possibly be in having stockpiled so many nuclear warheads that not only would one's opposition be obliterated but so would the rest of the world. It may have been an idealogical victory but in practical human terms it was suicide. It depressed me to think of all the strife that there was out there in the rest of the world. Where we were, there were no governments, no war, no nuclear threats, no terrorism, no party politics (apart from our own opinions), no denominational wrangling within a divided and seemingly crumbling church, no money and all the vices that go with the filthy lucre. There were just the four of us, miles from anyone else, totally at peace with our environment (in calm weather) and enjoying our situation (for the moment).

The day of the week was a Sunday, and like the previous few Sundays it felt just like any other day. Whilst we were sitting having a cup of cocoa in the Hotel Annex and listening to the radio, Julian tuned the radio to try to pick up something worthwhile. He picked up a BBC broadcast service from an Anglican church. It sounded dreadfully pompous and even horrible – a melange of unenthusiastic voices droning out the hymns as keenly as hanging out wet washing on a miserable Monday morning in February. I was glad Julian switched it off. I thought that a worship service should be just that – worship, adoration and praise. If the church wanted to have a lesson in praise then they ought to attend a pop concert. There girls could be seen and heard frantic for their idols for whom they would have done anything. Surely if non-Christian pop fans knew how to worship, how much more should Christians have known how to show their adoration of their Lord? Sadly, the lack of fire in the church in Britain could, I reasoned, be attributed to the fact that the basic relationship between the individual and his or her Lord was wrong. Where was the deep love? Where was the commitment? How God must have wept over Britain for the coldness and unfeeling nature of the Christian community in general. That service made me realise how much more important it was to be right in one's relationship with God in the first place, and then to praise and worship him in church or wherever, rather than just to attend a local service out of duty or pride or habit. It might fool one's fellow churchgoers but it would not fool God.

On the Monday morning radio sched, Barry the pilot informed us that he intended to evacuate Sledge Oscar first, leaving Sledge Hotel to mind the ice cores and report on the plateau weather to Rothera and the pilots. All four of us felt that such a plan was foolish as it would have left Tim and Julian without any means of emergency overland evacuation as the only 'doos were Peter's and mine and would have gone on the first flight. We discussed the plan further then decided to radio Rothera to tell them our views. We also felt that it would have been better if the Base Commander made the decisions rather than some trumped-up fly-boy as someone described him. Our weather was absolutely dingle and was quite warm, −14°C. However, Fossil Bluff and Rothera were manked in well and truly so there was to be no flying that day. Peter and Tim decided that they would try to climb Mount Charity while Julian and I did some more measurements. They set off on their climbing conquest at about 2 o'clock that afternoon and expected to be back by 8.30 that evening. Julian and I finished our work. Time ticked by. 8.30 came and went. Two hours later, well after the sun had set there was no sign of Tim or Peter. Their continued absence was beginning to cause Julian and I mild consternation. It was a very cold night; −25 degrees Celcius but at least it was calm. At 12.40 am, we heard two 'doos approaching. We were relieved that they had returned safely. They had reached a col slightly below the summit when Peter had had enough. Tim decided to continue alone and made it to the peak. Thankfully, their trip was completely without incident and they had had an excellent time.

The next day our weather was poor with low mank and strong winds. However, other sledge parties and the men at Fossil Bluff were successfully airlifted back to Rothera. We found out that Sledge Tango had depoted half their sledge unit (ie one 'doo and sledge) and were to be picked up by helicopter from HMS *Endurance*. What was worrying the Base Commander at Rothera was that the 'shut-off' date by which all sledge parties were to be back on base was that Tuesday, and there were still several parties out in the field. With winter approaching quickly, the likelihood of bad and unflyable weather was increasing.

The days came and went. Wednesday. Thursday. Friday. We were becoming increasingly vexed in our situation. The nights were becoming very cold indeed and life was proving to be more uncomfortable as the time went on. We started to think that the planes would never arrive and we would have to sledge out somehow. We had far too much clatch* to take it all out with us by 'doo. Our minds conjured with the options. After our last sledge journey Peter and I both hoped that a further trip like that would have been unnecessary.

I had been thinking a lot about Sue again. I really did not know what to make of our relationship. Perhaps it was not right for us to even think about an emotional involvement; Sue had all her concerts and missions, and I was thousands of miles away. That was not exactly conducive to any sort of relationship. 'Still,' I consoled myself, 'there is no point worrying about it. When I reach Rothera and see all the mail that will be waiting for me, I will know one way or another!' Perhaps it was good that we were not more deeply involved; if our relationship was not to work out, neither of us would feel hurt or disappointed. I was certain God had plans for both of us and that it was a matter for us to try to find out what those plans were. I recommitted our relationship to God and left Him to worry about it. Of one fact I was certain and that was that I was very fond of Sue.

As the week passed, we were becoming more despondent at our non-return to base. Saturday arrived and still no news from Rothera. The planes were busy picking up another sledge party but our weather was too poor for us to stand any chance of being picked up.

One of the major disadvantages of camping at nearly 7,000 feet altitude on an Antarctic ice sheet nearly in the austral winter was having to perform acts of nature outside. During a blow the wind chill factor made it feel like about

−45 degrees. To strip down to bare essentials was then a definite act of desperation and masochism. One squatted over a freshly dug hole facing the wind. Everything filled up with ground drift; the hole, one's crotch, one's trousers and underpants. Once the deed was done, it was a matter of standing up and fastening one's garments as quickly as possible and trying to do so without letting much freezing cold snow into the seat of one's trousers. Otherwise, back in the tent, the trapped snow melted and the unlucky Fid had to sit in wet garments which was most uncomfortable. There were lots of horror stories about unfortunate Fids who, not having faced the wind, consequently filled their trousers with unmentionables and, what was worse, did not realise it until they sat down again in the tent. Then there were reports of frost-nipped or fly-snagged genitals. The former a result of tardiness in the face of strong winds, and the latter, an over-eagerness in dressing to retreat to the tent. In really bad weather, we could not leave the tent in order to urinate, so we kept an old meat tin for just that purpose, referred to as the pee-tin. The heat of the liquid, when disposed of, melted a deep hole so the waste was kept a good distance down in the snow. If there was any doubt about hygiene, a good scoop of snow covered over the rubbish so there was no odour.

One activity which was much appreciated by us all was Julian's culinary efforts at making such things as 'chocolate lurk' which turned out like stodgy chocolate porridge, and pancakes which ended up like runny scrambled egg. Despite their ghastly appearance they tasted very nice.

At 5 pm that Saturday, Julian and Tim went off to their tent to do a radio sched with Rothera. When they returned they reported that Barry was flying our way and would be with us in fifty minutes. Peter and I could not believe it. We thought Julian was joking and we ended up splitting our sides with laughter. We all trouped back to the radio with Julian to listen to the banter. Shortly after we heard that Barry had had to turn back to Rothera because of the mank.

When we came up on the 7.30 pm sched, we spoke to Barry and not to Flo'. Unfortunately, Barry implied that we were not doing our met. obs. correctly and even fabricating our reports. Peter, who did not like Barry at the best of times, took the handset and told him exactly what he thought of him and where he could stick his met. obs. When he had finished the rest of us gave Peter a round of applause for his tirade. It made us all feel better.

At dinner absolute hilarity and lunacy reigned. We could hardly eat our meal for stomachs hurting through too much side-splitting laughter. By the end of the evening we were exhausted. Julian's comment that 'the plane would arrive in fifty minutes' was voted joke of the month.

When I walked back to Sledge Oscar's living tent at the end of the day, I saw a most magnificent sunset. It looked as if it would be dingle next day.

We duly awoke to a brilliant morning, had a prompt breakfast and were told that the weather was flyable at Rothera so all systems were go for our evacuation. Both planes would be with us in an hour or so. We very quickly readied the tents, sledges and 'doos, working hard in shirt-sleeves and feeling hot despite the temperature being $-15°$.

At 9.30 am two tiny specks could be seen in the sky, growing larger by the second. Moments later one plane approached and landed aggressively, not wanting to waste time taxiing. The other plane circled slowly and landed miles away before taxiing in to our camp. Within an hour, everything bar the large boxes of ice cores was loaded on board the two aircraft. The Director of BAS was acting as co-pilot on the first plane and he mucked in with everyone else, carrying heavy boxes and tidying up. Peter and I boarded the first plane; I found myself a niche next to one of the starboard windows so I had a good view as we flew north and west. Rees, our pilot, turned the Twotter and we could feel the plane rock as it carefully slid over some sastrugi. The throttles were pushed forward and the power surged to the propellers. We inched off quickly gathering speed. The rough bumping as the plane rushed over the snow surface suddenly ceased as we lifted off. We were finally on our way home. The visibility out of my window was excellent and I had a magnificent view over the peaks that made up the Eternity Range, and then over the mountains on the west side of the Antarctic Peninsula as we made our way to Adelaide Island and to Rothera. The air was so clear we could easily make out the crevasses on the glaciers which streamed around nunataks which, from our altitude, appeared like mere pimples on the icescape below. White icebergs contrasted with the blue sea in which they drifted. The whole scene looked as if it was static, with nothing moving or likely to change. In reality that was far from what was happening. The ice was perpetually on the move, the sea was a veritable hive of activity and motion, and as Peter and I had found out on our memorable sledge journey, when the weather was bad, the scene could change dramatically within seconds. From the aircraft we had a feeling of being removed from that environment, of becoming remote from the intimate relationship we had had whilst under canvas. That plane journey marked not only the end of my main field season, but also another change of lifestyle.

9: Return of the Wanderers

The flight to civilisation took about an hour. We circled over Rothera giving us an excellent aerial view. The plane started its descent turning in over Reptile Ridge and onto the skiway. Rees landed the Twotter very smoothly and taxied towards a bright red caboose, the only shelter at the air facility. The plane's back doors were opened and we were greeted by two of the air mechanics. Peter and I unloaded the plane as quickly as we could as Rees had to fly back to Mount Charity Depot to load up the remaining ice-core boxes, thus clearing out Sledge Hotel and Sledge Oscar completely. Everyone would then be back on base, some five days late. Just as our plane had been refuelled, the other plane with Barry piloting arrived. Peter and I were left to sort out our gear on our own. I felt that until we had returned all our kit and equipment safely down to base ourselves we had not really finished our field season properly. Once our sledges had been reloaded and securely lashed, we set off towards the base. Peter led the way and I followed with my 'doo. We came to a part of the short journey called 'the traverse' which comprised travelling along the foot of Reptile Ridge just below a bergschrund*. The snow there was steeply cambered and considerable care had to be exercised in order not to lose control of the vehicles which could all too easily have toppled over. The route over this ground was marked by old oil drums and stakes. To venture outside these markers would have put one at risk of encountering one of the many crevasses in the area. Under fair contrast there was little doubt as to where the roadway was as it was heavily rutted by the tracks of snowcats* and muskegs* as well as other 'doos. A standard way of skidooing along the traverse with a fully laden sledge was for one 'doo to lead pulling the sledge which was also roped to the front of the second 'doo which acted as a brake. Carefully we edged our way along the steep slope as far as the top of the 'ramp'. This was an ice wedge which provided the only access from the top of the glacier, on which the skiway was situated, to the base which was nearly at sea level. We had to stop before descending the ramp in order to wrap chains around the sledge runners so as to act as additional brakes whilst we went down the precariously steep and icy slope. The snow cover had all but disappeared and blue ice had been bared by recent warm rain. Once at the bottom of the ramp we unhitched the sledge and returned to the far end of the traverse to repeat the whole process with the second sledge. This time, I led the way down with Peter on the trailing 'doo. Leading was far easier than being on the second 'doo. When we reached the bottom, Peter came over to me and said, 'There's more to being second man than I thought! I am sorry for what I said to you on the Armstrong.' I thought that that was real vindication and definitely made up for any previous altercation.

With all our kit safely returned to base, Peter and I headed off for some lunch. It seemed very odd to see so many people, many of whom I did not know. I felt ill at ease at first. Dave, the Base Commander was relieved that we had been safely airlifted at last and handed us each a wodge of mail which we eagerly sorted through. There were two letters from Sue, several from my parents and my sister, a pile of letters from a class of primary schoolchildren in Cambridge, and one from someone who had heard a letter of mine being broadcast on a popular magazine programme on BBC Radio 2. The letters from the children were splendid fun to read. They each enclosed yet more penguin jokes and pictures that they had drawn. I did enjoy reading Sue's letters, and I reread them over and over again. They made up for all the doubts that I had had, the fears that I had felt and the uncertainties that I had experienced. It was not that the letters were particularly passionate but they were just what I needed at that time, newsy letters from a very dear friend which made me feel all the more keen to see Sue again.

After all my outdoor work was finished for the day, I was allowed to have a shower, my first for two months. This was as much by popular request of the other men on base whose noses reminded them all too poignantly of our need for a wash! The heat of the water made my skin tingle and I felt fresher by the minute. There were marked bands around my wrists and my neck where my skin had been exposed to the elements and two other pale patches, one over each eyelid. This effect was known as the panda look, although in reverse. Wearing snow goggles to protect my eyes had kept my eyelids from becoming browned like the rest of my face. After my shower I felt like a revitalised person. I almost did not recognise myself in the mirror. After all I had not seen my reflection since the start of the field season.

Dinner that evening was a real feast in comparison with field rations, even with goodies. I retired to my bunk quite early. That night I slept very badly; I was so hot. The base was heated to a comfortable 20°C, but being some 40 degrees warmer than we had been used to, it was like walking straight into a hot sauna. In time I reacclimatised and lost my resistance to the cold. I had also not realised that I had lost about seven pounds in weight due primarily to dehydration. Yet a few days later that weight had returned.

My first breakfast on base was a feast in comparison with our field ration of porridge. It was very strange to have to eat with some forty or so people. I felt very overcrowded. Although the food was good and the company convivial, there were times when I had had enough and wanted to be outside on my own. I needed time to readjust to dealing with people again. I was missing the vast open space of George VI Ice Shelf and of the plateau, the great expanses of deserted unpopulated wilderness unspoilt by man. Base represented an intrusion by man into that fragile environment. With a permanent base came dirt, pollution, noise, death (for some animals such as seals). We were aliens in a foreign world and yet we were acting as if we owned it and ruled it. Having so recently returned from the field I found that hard to accept. Surely we were there fighting for survival more than the penguins and seals for they had adapted wonderfully to their environment; they had no choice. We had consciously decided to leave our normal habitats and entered one for which we were very poorly equipped as creatures. We had to surround ourselves in our own artificial environment. We were totally dependent upon the supplies we brought with us, and yet we did all that to satisfy some academic curiosity or political objective. How mixed our motives were for being there. The society within that base complement was a microcosm of what we had left behind in England or wherever. There were cliques and an apparent hierarchy, some of which was a result of the odd combination of staff recruiting; some staff were permanent employees and were normally the senior staff (Perma-Fids*) whilst most men were on fixed term contracts. All the support staff (cooks, radio-ops, generator electricians, builders, GAs, etc) were on contracts as were all the non-Perma-Fid research staff. Consequently, the Perma-Fids tended to keep aloof from the Fids and did fewer of the less messy or unpopular chores. Some, however, cut across their Perma-Fid status and mucked in with everyone else which improved their reputation on base. A degree of antagonism existed between those men who had wintered and those who were 'summer only'. In addition there was inter-disciplinary rivalry; geologists jibed at the glaciologists because of the large volume of clatch* that they needed to do their work and yet conveniently forgot that they collected tonnes of rock specimens, far outweighing glacio-clatch, a fact with which the glacios used to counter the geos. GAs sometimes resented the scientists, especially as the latter were better paid. There was still the element of hierarchy through professional status: research staff were at the top, research assistants in the middle, GAs next, then the general support staff at the bottom. Fortunately, there was little emphasis placed on that on our base but it did raise its ugly head at times on the American station Palmer. In many respects it was good that there were no women on base for no doubt there would have been a strong element of sexual competition amongst the men for the favours of the women, and it would have provided another not inconsiderable stress with which to cope.

As I was a summer-only Fid, my presence on base was strictly temporary and there was barely time to fit into the routines on base. However, I tried my best. Within a couple of days of returning to Rothera, I was put onto gash guties which kept me out of mischief for the day.

My main responsibility on base was to finish my research work and write up a field season report which would then be sent back to BAS with those people flying back to England. So for much of the first few days I was ensconced in the library endeavouring to type up some results of my experiments and to say what I had achieved during the season. When I was not involved in my report writing, I helped out with building work around the base, painting, roofing, some concreting, and later building a large fuel tank. I was also fortunate in being able to spend almost two weeks carrying out some electrical experiments up at the airstrip on the glacier there. I was able to commute by skidoo to where the caboose was each day. It was a very civilised way of carrying out my research.

One important aspect of being back on base after what had been a very hectic field season was the relaxation. After dinner each evening there would be a film or slide show. When the weather was reasonable, several of us went skiing on the ramp. Several Fids would drive 'doos as ski-lifts whilst the remainder attempted to ski down the steep slope without falling over. My first Saturday evening back on base proved to be very memorable as 'Big Mac', the base cook, decided to prepare a barbecue for evening scradge. It was hardly surprising that after a short while back on base I had put on a considerable amount of weight.

One fine evening I decided to go for a stroll up the ramp for a bit of peace and quiet, and privacy. The view from the top of the ramp was sensational. I could make out the mountains of northern Alexander Island which were over 125 miles to the south. The sun tinged pink the snowclad peaks on the mainland and the islands in between. In contrast, the freezing sea was greeny-grey with pale blue ice floes and white icebergs. Nestling below the ramp were the buildings of the base which looked so small when compared with what I could see.

As time progressed I was developing a distinct dislike for two of my colleagues. One was the base doctor who spent most of his time drunk or sleeping it off. He won the Golden Blanket Award, given to the Fid who spent the most time in his pit. Then there was 'P.J.', a colleague scientist who was voted 'Megamouth of the Year' for his incessant self-opinionated talking. I tried as much as possible to keep out of their way so as to avoid confrontation. One of my hideaways was in the potting shed where there was a glaciology laboratory. I would take a portable tape recorder and a couple of music tapes and settle down to read a book or do some letter writing in private. I would work well whilst listening to most music but when it came to Brahm's Fourth Symphony, I would stop work and think back to when Sue and I went to the Royal Festival

Hall in London. Amongst the pieces we hard there was that very symphony. Such pleasant memories!

During the time I was working up at the airstrip, several people went for day trips sledging with the huskies to savour the experience of dog-powered travel. One day, I watched as a dog team was readied. The dogs barked in their eagerness for the off, for they loved nothing better than to work hard. The sledge driver was a GA called Tim, a man with considerable sledging experience. Once all the dogs were ready, Tim gave the command to start 'Up dogs . . . weet' and off they went following close on the heels of the noisy snowcat. Tim kept the dogs on track by shouting more commands at them. Within only a few minutes the dog team and the 'cat were over the top of the ramp and out of sight.

One afternoon, part of my duties was to feed the 'men', ie, the huskies, with Tim 'the Brush' (a painter). I had to drive a dumper truck down to the spans and to the meat box where we were to load up chunks of seal meat. I stopped the dumper and picked up the metal claw for snagging the meat chunks and opened the lid. The smell of rotting flesh hit me and almost made me vomit. I glanced inside to see the bright red blood-stained food. I plunged the claw inside and started lifting out four-pound blocks. Once, I plunged the claw inside and felt a squelch before the metal spike dug home. When I lifted the claw out I saw that I had spiked a seal's head through one of its eyes. The sight made me gag. That was the one job I hated most, although it was an essential one if we were to keep on with huskies in the Antarctic Peninsula. One of the other jobs that, fortunately, I never had to do, was to go out seal hunting. Several of the men were used to doing it and were crack shots so the seals were killed quickly and efficiently. Nevertheless, I still would have preferred it if an alternative food supply could have been obtained for the dogs. At least the number of seals taken each year was strictly controlled. The whole issue of dogs on base was frequently the subject of hot debates amongst Fids. Some men were very much 'pro-dog' whilst others were 'pro-vehicle', but very few men, irrespective of their bias, could resist the photogenic husky pups.

The last week before RRS *Bransfield* was due to call involved much preparation. The base itself had to be ready for its annual resupply and so all the paper work as well as practical arrangements had to be completed. On a personal front, men returning home on board the ship were busy packing and making their final preparations. Others were frantically writing piles of letters, their last chance before the onset of their winter isolation.

As the ultimate week progressed so people's attention, including mine, turned increasingly to home. Fids could often be seen sitting on their own quietly contemplating their homecoming. My Antarctic voyage was two thirds over, but there was still another two and a half months to go before I was to see English soil again.

Before long, *Bransfield* was expected to arrive in South Bay. She had successfully sailed south from Faraday through pack ice and was rounding the southern point of Adelaide Island. I spent that morning sewing patches on my sledging anorak to repair gaping holes formed by acid burns when I had been carrying a lead-acid battery. We were all looking forward to the mail that she had on board. Perhaps there would be several letters for me from Sue. I lived in hope.

At morning smokoh, morale was high. Those who were leaving would do so soon, and those staying over winter would be rid of the rest of us, and free to settle down to a winter on their own. Flo' walked into the scradge palace with a long glum face. He hesitated then announced that *Bransfield* had run aground seven miles to the south of Rothera. We all laughed at the joke, thinking it was a good ruse for the last day on base. However, Flo' was not joking.

The high humour turned quickly to a state of nervous agitation. 'You've got to be kidding!' someone interjected. Flo' then told us that we ought to go up to the point near the flagpole and look for ourselves. Seconds later the scradge palace was emptied as everyone donned their jackets and boots and rushed as fast as they could to the vantage point. Sure enough, there in the distance was a ship, its bright white superstructure and distinctive red hull easily visible. What could also be seen was that the ship was listing markedly to starboard. Some people took long focal length lenses and photographed the ship; others found the prospect of a sinking ship too much to look at and returned to base, their heads hung low in despondency. *Bransfield* had burst one fuel tank and ruptured part of her outer hull. Some people in an effort to look on the lighter side said that all they wanted was the mail. One man in the lounge flattened a cardboard model of a ship with his fist in his frustration. As the day progressed the weather deteriorated along with morale. At high tide during the early afternoon, *Bransfield* floated off the rocks and limped into South Bay. By then it was snowing hard and there was a strong wind and strengthening. Later the mail was brought ashore and taken to the scradge palace where everyone hung around like vultures, waiting for their letters. Several of us sorted out the mail and Fids soon were walking off clutching a bundle of letters and assorted parcels. After all the post had been given out, the base was littered with Fids in a wide variety of nooks and crannies reading their letters in some semblance of privacy. Some men were laughing, others looked serious, whilst the odd wet eye was visible. A couple of men had been chinged* by their muffin* and had taken the news very badly and wandered around puzzled and cross, frustrated that they were powerless by their remoteness to do anything about it. A couple of others had suffered the same fate but were visibly relieved – becoming dangerously close to wedding bells and an end to their freedom. In my pile of correspondence, I had two letters from Sue. My anticipation through the field season of a warm letter with hope for a developing relationship with Sue was dashed. Although she had written lovely newsy letters, they did not tell me what I wanted to know, how she felt about me. I was perplexed and knew no better where I stood with her. Peter had received the letter he had been anxiously waiting – Joan had accepted his marriage proposal. He went around in a lovelorn stupour clutching the letter to his chest and sighing. Folk teased him but he was oblivious. After dinner, most of us sat around reading letters and telling others our news and showing off the latest pictures of our womenfolk.

The weather had really deteriorated with strong winds whistling the heavy falls of snow into rapidly growing drifts around the buildings. I decided to nip over from the main building to the potting shed even though the conditions were atrocious and I was only wearing my light indoor clothes and footwear. Half way between the two buildings I slipped and fell completely over. Within seconds the snow had blanketed me. Quickly I stood up and more carefully found my way to the labs. The thought of what could have happened if I had hit my head and been stunned for a while crossed my mind. Hypothermia could easily have set in and with the speed with which the snow was falling, I might not have been found for days. My lesson had been learned. That experience warned me that although I was safely on base, outside was still a dangerous environment and one which deserved considerable respect. No one could afford to have adopted a contemptuous attitude to their surroundings. That was as true around the base as it was high up on the plateau of the Antarctic Plateau. It was all too easy to be lulled into a false sense of security; mistakes under such inhospitable conditions could have been fatal.

With so many men on the base many of whom I did not know at all well, there were times when I felt more isolated there than at any time out in the field. It made me realise that in ordinary life back home, that feeling of isolation was a very real problem for some people. For example, walking into a crowded restaurant and having to sit and eat all alone, served to intensify that loneliness. It was a sad fact that often the acutest loneliness was not through physical or geographical isolation, but could be felt in the middle of a crowd, surrounded by people who did not care about you. If you were suddenly not to exist, no one around would lament your passing. That kind of problem was one that I thought was increasing back home in our modern society.

To relieve the congestion on base, many of us were to transfer to *Bransfield* in the morning for the ship to be our home for the coming few days or weeks. *Bransfield* moored out in South Bay and Fids commuted to and fro by the motor launch.

After my last night on base, I did not feel any sadness at leaving, as I was still very much in the Antarctic. The transfer from land to ship marked the start of my journey northwards. I was no longer a raw Fidlet; my experiences over the field season had given me new confidence both within my work and, more importantly, within myself.

10: The Rescue

After *Bransfield* had moored and staff had come ashore, we asked them what it felt like on board during the grounding. Apparently, when the ship hit the submerged reef for the first time, everyone jarred on impact. Those sitting in the Fiddery were dislodged from their seats, but there was little panic. The lads on board just thought that the ship had powered her way through heavy brash ice and collided with a huge floe. It was only when they realised that there was no sea ice anywhere near the ship that it dawned on them what had happened. Their reaction was quite calm and was typically British: there was a general call for 'a fresh cup of tea. The grounding was quite serious. The ship had dislodged the rock which she first struck, glanced off and then grounded on another part of the reef. Such were the hazards of carrying out soundings in uncharted waters. News of the grounding reached HMS *Endurance* at Port Stanley, which then 'leaked' the news to the world's press before sailing proudly south, obviously pleased that she was justifying her presence in the South Atlantic.

MV *Hero* had also heard the news and responded. This was a tiny trawler which had been chartered by the National Science Foundation as a resupply vessel for Palmer Station. On board were some experienced ex-US Navy divers who had offered to inspect the damage to *Bransfield's* hull. *Hero* arrived a day later and the two divers were soon in action. They spent a considerable amount of time swimming down in the clear cold water making notes on special underwater boards. They informed us that the outer hull had been gashed in several places and one whole plate had been ripped open and bent double. Undoubtedly, after some telling a degree of embellishment crept into the damage report. Thankfully, the ship was still seaworthy and could continue with her itinerary but would obviously have to be checked out.

The whole episode had a ring of irony about it. At the beginning of the season we had been laughing at the demise of the tourist cruise liner after her grounding, and now the *Bransfield* was like a sieve after her rocky encounter. It was a case of he who laughs last laughs longest.

While the damage assessment was being undertaken, the relief of Rothera Base was under way. There were tons of food and supplies for us to unload and there were thousands of gallons of fuel to discharge. In worsening weather conditions it was often hard to see the *Bransfield*. During one afternoon, visibility decreased so rapidly that within five minutes, all one could see was a few yards ahead. *Bransfield* was completely obscured but the relief continued. I spent much of my time manhandling crates and boxes onto pallets for shifting by the ship's crane to the small scow and thence to the shore.

Several of *Hero's* crew came aboard *Bransfield* on the first evening to have a few jars of beer. Most of our visitors were very pleasant and appreciative and offered us a reciprocal visit aboard *Hero*, which we duly accepted. One *Hero* crewman had obviously had too much to drink. He introduced himself as 'Big Al Supercook – the best cook the world has ever seen'. With this modest introduction he then went on with similar diplomacy and grace shouting in his inebriated southern drawl: 'If it wasn't for us Yanks where would you . . . Limeys be now? At the bottom of the sea where you deserve to be. Aren't you . . . Limeys lucky having us Yanks come and save you?' No one dared to argue. His colleagues tried to placate him and directed him back to his own vessel, profusely apologising for his antisocial behaviour. Everyone was relieved once he had left.

The following day, the relief of Rothera was completed and *Bransfield* was readied for departure. For some of my colleagues, it was time to bid a fond farewell to the base which had been their home for over two years. The compelling urge to return home overcame any tinge of sadness at leaving. Many were pleased to be on their way at last. Those of us who had spent only the summer south could not feel the same depth of feeling towards our departure from the base. After all, I had spent far more of my time in a tent miles from anywhere and my sojourn at the base had always felt very transient. I had my research back in Cambridge to which to look forward, and then there was Sue and the thought of her soon dispelled any disappointment at having to leave to sail north.

MV *Hero* left for Palmer Station during the morning. *Bransfield* weighed anchor and was under way in the early afternoon. As she turned to leave South Bay, she sounded her hooter and blared out her farewell to the wintering complement who could be seen standing near the flatstaff on the promontory, waving. They would not see another soul until the following spring with the arrival of the Twin Otters at the start of the next summer field season. It did not take long for the ship's new arrivals to sort themselves out. The Fiddery was soon host to men with their noses buried in books, playing chess of just idly chatting or supping at drinks. We were bound for Faraday to pick up a few more Fids to take them home. As we sailed north we met the HMS *Endurance* so that she could escort us back to Port Stanley. Apparently the plight of *Bransfield* had reached the national news on TV and radio in Britain. The two small red ships were famous but for a while.

We anchored overnight near the Argentine Islands while we had business at Faraday Base. That evening I was sitting in the Fiddery reading a book when someone glanced out of the starboard window and commented on how low the clouds were. Those slow moving clouds were quickly identified as an iceberg, and it was only a few yards off our side. Moments later, the ship lurched as something ground against the metal flanks of the ship. We had been struck by an iceberg. We dashed out to see what had happened. As we arrived the outline of the back of a drifting iceberg faded into the evening. The ship's stern deck was covered with tons of ice which had fallen from the passing giant. The stanchions supporting the helicopter deck were buckled and the red side plates of the hull had been dented. Thankfully the impact had been confined to only a glancing blow above the waterline. We set to with shovels to rid our ship of its icy load. The twisted metal would have to wait for more substantial treatment later.

The following morning *Bransfield* and *Endurance* were under way again. As we sailed slowly through the Lemaire Channel, we were treated to a spectacular sight of 150 seals swimming as fast as they could across our bows several hundred yards ahead of us. On some of the ice floes we could make out the distinctive head shape of some leopard seals, which were famed for their ferocity. Seeing their enormous teeth and jaws to match, such notoriety seemed very plausible. One seal was lying on an ice floe not far from the path of the ship. I was surprised to see one of the cabin stewards, a lad still in his teens, take a beer can and hurl it as hard as he could at the seal. Fortunately he missed. It was a case of unwanton hooliganism. A fellow steward, equally young, was just about to do the same with his beer can when several of us shouted at him to stop. They turned and rudely gesticulated at us and walked off.

Once north of the Lemaire Channel we sailed east of Anvers Island, and passed Damoy on Wienke Island. Our next destination was an Argentinian base to pick up some scientific equipment which had been used in a joint research programme. After the official shore party had completed their work at Almirante Brown, we were invited to look around the base. In their small mess room we were treated to thick black coffee, cognac and biscuits. The base was a real contrast to any of the British bases; the rooms were small and dingy with dark narrow passages leading between rooms. I was glad that I did not have to stay in such conditions. As we left the small jetty in our launch, our Argentinian colleagues stood and waved us goodbye. We felt sorry for them in that they had such inadequate facilities for either research or comfortable living. However, our visit had been a valuable experience.

We set sail on *Bransfield* during mid-afternoon. All that was left for us to do was to sail to Port Stanley on the Falkland Islands. That evening after dinner I felt depressed for no apparent reason. What was weighing me down to some extent was a feeling of being distant from the Lord. I was still reading my Bible daily but I was not stopping to think things through or learn from any of the study notes I used. Perhaps I was suffering from *Bransfield* lassitude. As I read my Bible that evening I found the truth of a verse in Philippians very helpful: 'And with all his abundant wealth through Christ Jesus, my God will supply all your needs.' (Phil. 4, 19; GNB). I applied that to my thinking about my relationship with Sue. God knew what we both needed at that time as well as what we both wanted, but how difficult it was at times to distinguish honestly between wants and needs.

The following day was notable for not only yet more spectacular scenery as we sailed northwards, but also for the sight of a Sie whale blowing not far from the ship. It soon disappeared from view slipping effortlessly below the surface. During the day the weather deteriorated and the sea state worsened. The ship pitched and rolled quite gently but sufficiently to cause many of us to retreat to our bunks to lie down. Conditions stayed poor for the next day and a half. The Fiddery was deserted most of the time, populated only by Fids with strong stomachs or very good sea legs. Not being one of them I only surfaced long enough to dash into the scradge palace, eat my meal and rush back to my bunk without being sick. At one point *Bransfield* was steaming too fast for *Endurance* which had fallen behind us. She radioed for us to slow down as it would not have been proper etiquette for the ship which was bring rescued to precede her rescuers. *Endurance* overtook us and then proceeded to steam around in circles to waste time as we were ahead of our estimated time of arrival. After all, it was not done to arrive at one's destination before one's ETA and, besides the Captain had not finished his lunch.

Right on time, *Endurance* led the way into Stanley harbour. The sun was shining brightly in a clear blue sky and there was hardly any wind at all, somewhat unusual for Stanley harbour. Within minutes of dropping anchor, a customs man came aboard along with a sack of mail. I had scored a bumper crop of letters, including a superb letter from Sue. I could not open the envelope fast enough. As I opened the letter the aroma of perfume wafted out; the scent was deliciously female. The contents of the letter were no disappointment either. She had liked the flowers that I had ordered for her on Valentine's Day and she reckoned I was 100 per cent crazy. I had several letters from home and other good friends of mine. Inevitably I also received a bill – was there anywhere in the world where such hated things would not reach one? I also had a letter from someone in Australia who had read an article which I had published in the *Geographical Magazine* and had sent me news cuttings on related topics. The article had been about the use of icebergs as a source of fresh water for arid regions, such as western Australia. It felt good to know that my work was being read so widely. My first evening in Stanley was spent letter writing. It was good to recover quietly and fully from the rough sea journey. Tomorrow was a new day and there would be plenty of time to go ashore and explore.

11: Stanley and Friends

On the morning after our arrival from the Antarctic Peninsula, Derek (the dentist), Jerry and I decided to walk over the hills around Port Stanley. We took the first launch and were soon walking along the front from the jetty. Short rows of tin-roofed houses lined the roads. The small front gardens were neat and well looked after. Many a window displayed patriotic posters. 'God bless the Queen', and 'Keep the Falklands British' as well as many a Union Flag. A large seagull landed on an old cannon which proudly pointed over the water by the quayside as we passed by the red bricked cathedral with its whalebone archway. We saw the few shops that were there and, within minutes, we had reached the southern outskirts of the town. We came across the Governor's grand residence with its pristine lawns and tidy driveway. As I walked along the road I found it strange having to concern myself with kerb drill again after four months without it. The only traffic was old Land Rovers with their distinctive Falklands number plates. Once past the Governor's house and the War Memorial, our route took us past the Royal Marines barracks. Thereafter the road petered out and turned into a track as we headed towards the twin peaks of the Two Sisters which overlooked Stanley harbour. We climbed gradually, crossing over peat bogs and marshy areas until we reached the western summit of the two. There we stopped for a break. From our vantage point we could see virtually the whole town. Out in the harbour we could see *Bransfield* moored, and not far away, *Endurance*. The water was streaked with white lines where the wind whistled over it.

After smokoh we turned eastwards and scrambled over the second of the twin peaks of the Two Sisters. From there we walked across the valley. It felt good to be able to walk over grass again after spending four months seeing nothing but ice and bare rock; the greenery of shrubs and plants was refreshing. It made me realise how much we took such simple pleasures for granted, failing to appreciate the scenery around us in Britain. The walk was also a welcome respite from the confines of the ship. In rough weather, it was hardly safe to go for a walk up on deck even if one felt up to it. Instead we were confined to stay inside, and after a scrub-out the place smelt like a public lavatory. To be out in the fresh air and in the open space was a great feeling. The solid unmoving rock felt good beneath our feet. After lunch we walked up to Mount Tumbledown from which we could see over to the eastern coast and to the new road that was being built from Port Stanley to Darwin. We spent some time rock climbing on Mount Tumbledown. Before long we decided to walk down to the new road where we turned northwards back towards Port Stanley. Three miles later we were back at the jetty waiting for a launch to take us back to *Bransfield* and to a rejuvenating shower to ease aching feet.

That evening, Simon, a fellow glaciologist, Jerry and I had farewell drinks in my cabin. Simon was due to leave from Stanley to commence his jolly* through South and Central America before returning home to England. In fact the plane that was to fly him out the following day had landed at Stanley airport during the afternoon bringing with it some more mail. I had a further three letters which were from members of my family, all of whom had heard about *Bransfield's* grounding on the national news. My sister wrote that she strongly suspected I had been 'driving' at the time of the accident.

The following morning we said our farewells to those who were leaving the ship. I went into town to post my many letters, and also sent off thirty three films for processing back in Britain. Surprisingly, it was cheaper to send all my mail from Stanley than it would have been to have waited and posted it all from Cambridge.

After lunch, Stanley Radio announced that *Bransfield* was due to field a team for a soccer match against the Port Stanley Ladies XI. The referee was a junior officer from *Bransfield* but he was even more partisan than we had expected. If there was any cause to suspect foul play he always gave the advantage to the ladies. There was a considerable amount of attempted manhandling of the opposition by the ship team which was severely penalised by the referee. In the end, we lost by eight goals to two. Everyone had great fun.

After dinner on board ship, Peter, a radio operator, Vic, an electrician from Rothera, and I went into town to visit the Victory pub to see its English football league mementoes up on the wall, and the fire that was reputed to have been alight continuously for thirteen years. We then went over to the Rose pub where we stayed until closing time listening to several Fids playing guitars and fiddles. We played darts with an old Stanley resident and were soundly beaten by him.

The following day we walked to the lighthouse on Pembroke Point, and were given a guided tour by its keeper who told us proudly about its history and the technical details of the beautiful old light. We strolled back through tussock grass near the beach then back onto a track which took us to the airport road. We stopped off at the Victory Café where we were served by a very attractive Argentinian girl who had only been on the islands a week or so. We soon had to go back to the ship in order to prepare for a special cocktail reception that the Governor of the Falklands was giving *Bransfield's* complement that evening at his residence. Previous formal social functions had been horrendously superficial so I was not looking forward to this one.

After dinner, several of us caught the early evening launch to town and arrived slightly early at the Governor's residence. We were met at the door by a maid who showed us into a huge reception room. We felt very conspicuous in the middle of a deserted ballroom. A footman brought us drinks on a silver platter before the Governor and his wife entered and introduced themselves to us. As we chatted with them, more people arrived and the room started to fill. The footman and maids kept plying us with drinks, crisps, peanuts and dainty sausage rolls. Several of us thought that we ought to keep an eye on Vic during the evening as once he had had a few drinks there was no telling what he would get up to. At one stage a very attractive single woman introduced herself to me and we started chatting. I was beginning to think that cocktail parties were not such a bad idea after all. However, my conversation was short-lived and I ended up stuck with a real bore from Government House. Not long after I noticed that Vic was standing clutching a gin and tonic close to his chest and swaying backwards and forwards. His nose was red, his cheeks pink and his eyes were glazed. He was talking to a young woman from Government House and had a big mischievous grin on his gnome-like face. Suspecting trouble, I went over just as Vic turned to the woman and asked her whether she was good in bed. Without batting an eyelid she replied that he had better ask her husband who was standing next to her. Flummoxed and embarrassed by Vic's question, he stammeringly tried to change the subject. All was well for a while. However, some time later, Peter and I noticed that Vic was nowhere to be seen. We decided to go in search of him in case he was up to something. We went outside and we soon spotted him in silhouette against the streetlights at the end of the main drive. Vic was standing in the middle of the Governor's front lawn fumbling with his flies. 'Vic! No, don't! Stop! Not there!' we shouted, but it was too late. We heard him mumble a slurred 'Tha's berrer!' He was too used to the practice at Rothera of walking out of the main building down the gravel a few yards and relieving himself. After two years on base, it was going to take him a little while to become used to civilised habits. We decided that Vic had had enough and in his interests it was better if he was returned to the ship.

Once Vic was deposited safely in his cabin, I retired to mine. I had had enough of all the small talk. There seemed to be so much pretence there, people not wanting to reveal much of themselves or trying to present a false, more glamorous image. That reception was typical of how we tended to act in society, in formal functions, even in church meetings. Why were we all so coy of revealing our true nature? Did we have that much to hide? While on Base there had been no need for any masks; no one had anything to gain by not behaving naturally. Maybe we all want to be well thought of and liked, and throuch lack of confidence in our minds we start to act. It reminded me of a story I had heard of an accountant who, whenever he was asked what he did for a job, replied that he was a fireman. He made up some fantastic escapades and daring rescues. They were much more interesting than being stuck in a boring old office, number crunching. We did not go to that extreme, but I feared that most of us were guilty of some embellishment for effect. Status had a lot for which to answer in society.

The following day was a Saturday and in the afternoon there was a real sporting event, the annual rugby match between a *Bransfield* XV and Port Stanley XV. Rugby was not my game so I was quite content to spectate along with many other Fids and locals. The match was featured on Radio Stanley for the benefit of those who could not travel in to watch the game. Happily, the ship team won handsomely by sixteen points to seven. That evening, Stanley Youth Club had been invited to come aboard the ship to watch a film, Walt Disney's *Jungle Book*. The Fiddery was packed out with noisy screaming children and young people. After the film had ended the young people were treated to sticky buns and orange squash which disappeared extremely quickly.

On Sunday, three of us decided to try to attend a morning service at the cathedral but found out that there was only a Sunday school. Instead we later went to Evensong. It was conducted by a visiting vicar but unfortunately, neither the vicar nor the organist could agree on which tunes ought to accompany which hymn or chant. Consequently, the sung portions of the service were totally chaotic. After one verse of a hymn the vicar went over to the organist who stopped playing and then changed to a different tune. The vicar thought that all this was tremendously funny and ended up in fits of giggles. During a prayer he tried to stifle his guffaws with his handkerchief but his laughing had the better of him and he creased up and roared his head off. The congregation did not know whether to laugh with him or to protest at his disrespect. Then he confused the collections for Lent and Advent. It was difficult enough for me trying to follow the service in the Church of England prayer book as I was not familiar with it. The service left me feeling very sad and unsatisfied. I felt that it had been an insincere humanistic service, and that there had been so much missing from it. Where was the preaching of the Gospels, or the challenge of the Scriptures for contemporary Christianity? There was no mention of the reason for Christ's death on Calvary, or of conviction through his resurrection, and what about the power of the Holy Spirit? Sadly, the state of that church was not uncommon in Britain, nor was it confined to the Anglican church. It was no wonder that the popular image of the church was of a dying, powerless, ineffective body mostly supported by little old ladies who excelled when it came to tea parties and jumble sales. Where was the worldshaking leadership of the church within modern society?

Someone has made the comment that one reason why Britain has been going through so many troubles and a damaging recession is that the nation has turned from God. What is needed is not just an injection of money into the economy or increased overseas borrowing, but a sound investment in prayer. Until then, there will just be a decline until the nation comes to its knees. Britain has become a heathen nation with only a small minority going to church and an even smaller number being really committed. There is an increasing interest in witchcraft and the occult, especially by young people. The spiritual heart of our nation has been plucked out and replaced by superstitions and false beliefs rendering the nation no further advanced than when it was in the middle of the Dark Ages.

Those were depressing thoughts, but they made me feel determined to do something about it. Not that I could do much except make sure that I did not fall foul of the spiritual lassitude that was all too prevalent. That would be a start.

By the time the fiasco of the service was over, darkness had fallen. The night sky was clear and a myriad of stars was visible. Orion and the Southern Cross as well as the Milky Way could all be seen clearly. As we walked back to the ship I could not help but be reminded of the starlit skies that Sue and I had enjoyed seeing when walking along the South Bank of the River Thames in London. Those were indeed pleasant memories.

On Monday morning I decided to go for a stroll with one of my colleagues. As we were walking, an old Land Rover came by and stopped. The driver asked if we wanted a lift. We explained we were only out for a walk. He then invited us to join him peat digging. This was an activity we had never seen before so we readily agreed. Soon we were off the road trundling across rough ground. There in front of us were several deep trenches dug into the black peat. The old man explained as he started cutting that he had been a whaler and a seal hunter back in the 1930s. He had never been to the Antarctic Peninsula and had regretted it. He recounted some of his voyages and they made some of our recent troubles in storms mere trifles. He offered us the opportunity of cutting some peat. He made it look so easy that we agreed. In turn we picked up the spade and loaded on a peat block. Instead of lifting it adroitly over our shoulders and onto the pile near the Land Rover as he had done, we had trouble raising the peat above knee height. It must have weighed a good forty pounds or more, and yet the old man had thrown those blocks around as if they were only made of polystyrene. I was impressed by his fitness and strength and felt puny in comparison. During our conversation we raised the topic of sovereignty of the islands. Was the majority feeling still in favour of being British? He answered very strongly that some of the islanders felt more British than the British and that there was no question about to whom the islands belonged. However, he did voice a fear. He said it was not a question of 'if' the Argentinians invaded the islands but one of 'when?'. Tragically the answer to his question was to come no more than two years later when the streets along which I had walked that morning were full of Argentinian armoured vehicles and artillery and thousands of troops.

The next day was our last one in port and so it was time to walk through the lonely streets for a last look at the small town. On a wall of one tiny shop was a large painted picture of a penguin advertising trips to England and South America. Further on, I came across a very tidy little garden with its vivid green grass neatly cut. Flowers and shrubs filled the borders. All around the garden were smart painted ornaments. Many of the people I met during my walk I recognised and they acknowledged my greetings. Such was the size of the local community that it was easy to become acquainted with the locals. They always gave us a very warm welcome. I caught a launch back to *Bransfield* for the last time.

By early afternoon, all our farewells had been said. The launch was hoisted from the water and the gangplank raised. The crew busily set about preparing the ship for sea. One of the officers came down to the Fid deck and warned everyone to stow everything away securely as we were likely to encounter rough seas.

At 5 pm anchor was weighed, and *Bransfield* slowly turned to leave. She sounded her hooter and sirens many times in a noisy departure. As we passed *Endurance*, there was much Ensign dipping between the two ships. It was customary for a ship to partly lower her Ensign and then raise it again as a courtesy signal to naval vessels, irrespective of their nationality. We were finally off on the next leg of our voyage, bound for South Georgia.

12: Shackleton's Island

Our voyage to South Georgia took three days. As soon as we left the protection of the Falkland Islands the sea was rough but half way between the Falklands and South Georgia the weather improved. As we sailed east we noticed that we had several stowaways on board. A number of Snowy Egrets had been blown off course by the recent strong winds and had landed on the deck to rest. They were completely exhausted and one allowed itself to be picked up, brought inside and fed on bread and milk. A tiny Wilson's Stormy Petrel was also brought inside in an equally miserable state. It recovered quickly and was released unharmed.

One afternoon a school of porpoises swam alongside the *Bransfield* in very close proximity. They streaked along just beneath the surface, white patches on their black bodies clearly visible as they played nearby. What beautiful creatures, totally at one with their environment and so sleek and full of fun.

To help pass the time I had been reading an account of Sir Ernest Shackleton's epic voyage in 1914 from Elephant Island in the Antarctic Peninsula to South Georgia in only a small open boat. His considerable feat was accomplished in order to seek help for the remainder of his ship's crew who were still on Elephant Island. Unless he could gain another ship to sail south to rescue them, they would have perished. They had all become stranded after their ship, the original HMS *Endurance*, had been caught by sea ice, crushed and then sunk. As I was reading about Shackleton's exhausting march across the peaks of South Georgia to the little whaling station of Leith, I looked out of the window and saw those very mountains standing proud and awesome. I felt a great sense of admiration for those men. In many ways, my admiration for all the early Antarctic explorers of the beginning of this century, men like Scott and Amundsen, had increased enormously. Even with all my modern equipment I found the conditions in the Antarctic in summer physically and mentally very demanding, but what must it have been like for them? We had it easy by comparison. Nothing could detract from the feeling of admiration as I looked at those mountains across which Shackleton had struggled sixty six years before.

The view was memorable. Rising steeply out of the sea were the majestic peaks which comprised the spine of the island, summits clothed in white, glaciers creeping down their flanks amidst the velvet-like foothills with their veneer of vegetation. Around the ship a large number of birds swooped and whirled, a testament to the richness of the local environment.

By late morning we rounded a headland on the northern coast of the island and steamed into Cumberland Bay. At the head of the inlet was the old whaling station of Grytviken, all rusty and brown and obviously in a state of disrepair. We slowly inched our way closer to the rickety old jetty near the flensing plan*. Men from the base were there to greet us and to help with the mooring. Soon the lines were fast and the gangplank was down.

After lunch on board ship, several of us walked through the old whaling station, looking at the historic buildings. The wind rattled loose plates of corrugated iron which banged against metal stanchions. It was like a ghost town. Grass was growing through the wooden floors, the windows and doors hung limply on broken hinges, scrap metal lay everywhere. At one point I noticed a snow clad peak standing high above green foothills which stretched down to the station. The rusty old hulk stood as a memorial to what man could build. It had lasted less than 100 years. The mountain behind represented what nature could do; it had been there since before man walked on the face of this globe. That made me feel how insignificant man was. Despite our apparent mastery of our planet, we were powerless to control its processes and its immense forces. I wished other people could have had that perspective. If only the military minds would realise the fragility of our very existence on this planet, perhaps then they would think again about the foolhardiness of all the nuclear weaponry that was being stockpiled. Even if man annihilates his own kind, the world will continue, immeasurably changed but still existant. The countless billions of pounds being squandered on military munitions could easily provide for the well being of the whole population of our small world. Why should people starve or go without the basic medical care which we take for granted in the western world? The necessity for international aggression seems, to me, to be only in the minds of a tiny minority but one which controls the majority of world power. The demise of that whaling station was a portent of what could be. For many people such thoughts would have been totally depressing and demoralising, but for me I felt that our future depended even more then than ever on a return to God. I remembered why God had destroyed the known world in Mesopotamia in Noah's time. That flood which destroyed all but one family was as damaging in human terms as a nuclear holocaust would be today. That deluge was a result of a turning away from God. His promise to Noah was that never again would the world be destroyed by another flood (Genesis 9.11). The Book of Revelation however describes all too realistically wars and atrocities that could occur. Who was to know when Armageddon would happen? As far as I am concerned, I should concentrate on my relationship with Christ as only then will I know that I am living according to his will. There is nothing I can do to change the hearts and minds of those hell-bent on manufacturing weapons of greater and greater sophistication and destructive power, east or west. The only thing I can do is what God wants me to do, wherever that happens to me. For the time being it was on South Georgia.

We continued our walk beyond the whaling station, down to the beach where we came across numerous old whale bones and a solitary King Penguin, looking very regal in its black and silver-white garb with orange and blue-grey trimmings and beautiful dark blue eyes. Further along the beasch we met a group of elephant seals which were as impressive for their distinctive smell as they were for their enormous size. They snorted through ungainly noses and wallowed in a hollow amongst the tussock grass. These ellie* seals were some of the natural local residents of the bay and could be heart bellowing for miles around. Our final call on our walk was the grave and tombstone of the famous explorer, Sir Ernest Shackleton, who died on the island on January 5th 1922. His grave was covered in small metal plaques left by visiting members from ships of many different nationalities including East Germans, Poles, Russians and Argentinians. There were also wreaths of flowers laid carefully as marks of respect for the famous explorer.

I had only expected to stay on the island a few days and to sail with *Bransfield* when she went. However, when two of the overwinterers on the base found out that a glaciologist was on board, namely me, they requested of the Base Commander that I stay on the island to take charge of their glaciological programme for a month until *Bransfield* returned again. I was delighted to have the opportunity to stay on the island and to study some of the glaciers nearby.

That afternoon there was a special football match between a *Bransfield* team and one from the base; we played on a pitch which had pukka goal posts, touchlines and even a 'stand' for spectators. It was a close game but in the end the ship team lost by three goals to one.

The first night at Grytviken I spent on board ship having packed quickly in readiness for my stay on the island. The following morning I awoke bright and early. Several inches of fresh snow lay everywhere, and it was still snowing. The clouds were low and hid the upper portions of most of the peaks. Eight of us disembarked before the ship slipped her moorings and moved out into the bay. The sound of her loud hooter was the last we heard of her as she steamed out of the bay. We were then taken by launch across the inlet to King Edward Point where BAS had its base. The buildings at that point used to comprise the small township where the original Norwegian whalers and their families lived; there was a customs house, the Governor's house and a post office incorporating the magistrate's office as well as that of the harbour master, post master, and the registrar of births, marriages and deaths. The largest of all the buildings was the old hospital known as Shackleton House or 'Shack' House to its residents. The green-walled building had three floors; the top providing sleeping accommodation, the ground floor housing store rooms, drying areas, cloakrooms, a wet laboratory and various storage areas. All the public rooms were on the first floor as were two scientific wings, one for biological sciences and the other for atmospheric and solid earth geophysics. I was provided with a lab in the geophysics wing.

On our arrival the Base Commander gave us a chat about the base and the various no-go areas (for conservation and scientific reasons) and general safety instructions like fire and emergency boat drills. We were also issued with waterproofs as the island was particularly prone to wet weather. I was allocated a room with one of the Fids whose nickname was 'Mouse'. The view from our room was spectacular, looking out over the bay to the glaciers and snow clad peaks of the Allardyce Range. Many people would have paid thousands of pounds to see that view. For me, that was one of the perks of working for BAS, of having the opportunity of visiting places which had incredible beauty and scientific interest and yet were rarely visited by anyone. Mouse and a Dutchman called 'Hash' (no one could pronounce his real name) were to be involved with me in checking and re-establishing a stake network on a small glacier called Col, several miles to the south-east of the base.

Before dinner we retired to the bar and met a young French couple, Sally and Gerome, who were sailing around the South Atlantic and the Antarctic Peninsula in their yacht *Damien III*. They had made a very potent punch out of Brazilian rum, mineral water and passion fruit juice, and provided us with the white flesh and the milk from green coconuts.

After dinner I started to get to know some of the small group of Royal Engineers staying at the Governor's House. I was chatting to the major in charge and found out that it was his responsibility to examine the jetty at King Edward Cove and at Grytviken to see how much repair work was necessary. After dinner we were shown *The Revenge of the Pink Panther*, a film whose dialogue featured heavily in ordinary conversation on base. One or two of the Fids knew much of the script by heart and, true to Fid form, the hilarity of the evening was a consequence of their witty repartee.

That night I was able to sleep in a proper bed with sweet-smelling sheets and soft pillows. It was luxury after over four months of sleeping bags and ship bunks.

The next couple of days were spent in checking our mountaineering equipment in readiness for field work up on the glaciers. When our preparations were over Mouse and I set off to Glacier Col to stock up the small hut in readiness for a longer stay. We arrived and opened up the fibreglass navvies' hut that was to provide the only shelter for us. Inside it was dark and very cramped. The base of the wooden door had been eaten away by rats. At the far end were several shelves on which we could store food out of the reach of rodents. The bunks were just planks of wood about a foot wide, one on either side of the hut. There was no window and so the only source of light was a Tilley lamp, the heat from which caused the insides of the hut to condense up. We could of course open the door, but only if the wind was in the right direction, otherwise all the wind and snow blew right in. We soon realised that living in that hut was going to be a cold, damp experience.

After a quick lunch, we walked up to the glacier to check to see if any stakes were still standing. We found only a third of those that had been erected in a previous season and, of those, more than half had melted out and were lying on the surface. One stake had fallen into a small crevasse and had been broken. We completed our preliminary survey and returned via the hut to base.

With Sally on base I found myself thinking more about women. Whilst in the field it was all right; there were no women around, not even any pictures of them. But having met girls in the Victory Café, and at the Governor's reception, and now Sally, I found I was missing their company. The many girlie magazines on the BAS bases were an extra temptation. Even so, I had been out of England only four months; what must it have been like for those who had been out for two years? It was worrying that *Bransfield* was due to sail via Rio de Janeiro, where the women were supposed to be real beauties and very accommodating. I was going to have a real battle ahead, I could see. I prayed hard that if I was tempted, I would be given the strength to resist.

The weather remained bad for several days. After scrubout on the first Saturday four of us walked over to Grytviken in a wind which occasionally gusted up to eighty knots. We went to the Kino building to play badminton.

At first the creaks of the building did not concern us, but as the wind gusted, the whole building tilted over, groaning as it went. The inside shape changed from a cube to a rhombus and then back again. Several times we bolted for the doors thinking that the building was about to collapse around our ears. It was in Grytviken that I decided to cut off most of my beard; it had become very long and shaggy.

On the following Sunday the most southerly football club took to the field again. There were times when we were wallowing in a quagmire at one end of the pitch; it was no place to demonstrate one's fitness at ball control.

Monday morning marked the first day of a longer stay up at the hut at Glacier Col. Dave, an ionospherisist*, joined me. We spent the morning sorting out the hut, then scouted around the glacier and began our work. When we eventually returned to the hut the wind was gusting fiercely. As we lay on the ground shielding our eyes from the dust, we could see whirlwinds gyrating violently down the glacier and heading straight for us. The wind in these was even stronger than before. I looked up at the wrong time and was caught by one vicious vortex which rolled me over sideways and blew me along. I spread out my arms and legs as wide as I could to make it as difficult as possible to roll over but still I was buffeted until suddenly the wind died. If it had continued for much longer, I could have been blown over a cliff. As soon as the wind had abated, I stood up and ran back to the hut as did Dave. We had just recovered our breath when we heard yet more wind approaching from off the glacier. It sounded like a steam train thundering towards us and it hit the hut with an enormous bang sending everything on the shelves flying. A five-pound tin of meat plummeted down from the shelf, narrowly missing Dave's head. We could not hear each other even though we were shouting at the tops of our voices. Then, just as quickly as it had blown up, it died and left a strange, eerie, quiet. We stayed where we were for a while not certain whether another squall would strike. That night the wind did return. I lay in my sleeping bag wondering when the hut door would fly off. The windward side of the hut was taking a hammering not only from the wind but from the sand and grit being blasted against the thin walls. The whole hut creaked as it fought to withstand the onslaught. It was time for one of those emergency prayers – Help! However, by early morning, the wind had subsided.

In the next four days we managed to achieve most of our work schedule in fine but cold weather. One morning I accidentally stepped through a snow bridge over a small water-filled crevasse, falling in as far as my waist. The fall broke the straps on my crampon for my right boot, but otherwise, apart from being slightly surprised at my sudden descent, there was no damage done.

During the work I had come across an ice cave beneath the glacier. A small stream flowed in from one end and out of the other. It provided us with a good opportunity to study the underside of the ice.

Over the radio we heard that a Russian stern trawler, *Nikol Ostrovsky*, had moored at the jetty at Grytviken to take on water and her crew had beaten a home team at football by two goals to one!.

On the Saturday we returned to base. I then realised that the previous day had been Good Friday. It was to be a strange Easter for me. We found out that the storms we had had during our week up at Glacier Col had not left the base unscathed. They had recorded wind speeds of up to eighty four knots down in the sheltered bay and the Fids on base could well believe our reports of 120 knot gusts.

After a fish and chip supper for Saturday scradge, we were invited aboard the Russian ship. We were met at the gangway of the sombre grey coloured vessel by Andrei, who acted as our interpreter. He ushered us to the small officers' wardroom, where we were invited to seat ourselves around a huge table covered by bottles of wine, cognac, glasses, beer and various Russian food concoctions including raw fish. At 9 pm it was announced that we could eat Pascal bread which was a kind of sponge bread and was very tasty. The significance of the timing was that it coincided with midnight in Moscow. Afterwards we were taken to a general mess where very loud Russian music was played through a couple of loudspeakers. It sounded more like the accompaniment to the May march through Red Square rather than dance music. However, several of the younger members of the Soviet crew were prancing about in what one was given to believe was a dance, so after a while several of us joined in, more out of politeness than for any other reason. The Russian crew was mixed but some of the women were larger than the men! In one corner of the mess I spotted one little fellow who was quietly emptying a bottle of vodka on his own. He was momentarily overshadowed by a huge woman who then dragged him to his feet and waltzed him across the room. It was doubtful as to whether his feet actually touched the floor during any of this. It was not long until I and a couple of others were taken by a couple of Russian matelots down to one of the crew cabins where a private party was underway. The cabin was about half the size of one on the *Bransfield* and yet it was home for four men. In those cramped quarters we were treated to salami, fish, bread, paté, and of course to Russian vodka. It was quite a session with the Russians toasting 'Russia, England, friendship' and then downing a schnapps glass of vodka and then repeating the whole thing again and again. I retreated to the main party upstairs. There was a demonstration of some traditional Russian folk dances, and we tried to converse with our hosts. However, it was very difficult on two counts. Firstly, there was the obvious difficulty of the language barrier. Secondly, there was the

KGB Commissar. Everyone was subject to his authority, even the captain. Throughout the evening, whenever in his presence, the Russians all took their lead from him; no one drank before he did; no one danced before he did. They seemed to be in fear of him. In the main room we were surprised that the walls were painted bright red. There were notice boards on three of the four walls of the room; the fourth wall had windows. On those notice boards were policy statements of the Politburo, rules and regulations according to Marxist doctrine, and even photographs of all the politburo members. Andrei explained who was who, but there were two gaps where photographs had been removed. He skipped over these at first but was stopped by a Fid who pointed and asked about it. Andrei looked rather nervously around. The same Fid said 'Soviet heart problems strike again, eh Andrei?' and the Russian nodded quickly. These two unfortunate unknown Politburo members must have fallen from favour and had been removed, either by internal exile or permanently by the all-too-common 'heart attack'. Our Russian hosts were most generous. They insisted on giving us each small enamel lapel badges of Lenin; I ended up with three different ones depicting the Russian leader. A fourth one featured a red flamed torch on a blue background with the years 1944 and 1974 and the Russian for Sebastopol, the home town of our hosts. They also wanted us to sign books and pennants. They presented our base with a superb picture showing Davey Jones' Locker burnt into wood, and a beaten copper panel hand made by the captain showing a figure of a woman and a rose. One Russian took one of my colleagues aside in a corridor and furtively pulled out a small icon from inside his shirt which he then thrust into the Fid's hand and rushed off, not wanting to be spotted. A religious icon was a treasured item and was not given lightly. If the man had been seen by the Commissar he would have been in trouble. Andrei would not let us leave the ship until he had played us some tunes on his guitar and had sung us some songs. They were dreadful. When eventually we tried to leave, everyone was eagerly shaking our hands and waving us goodbye. It had been a very interesting and eye-opening experience for most of us.

The following afternoon the *Nikol Ostrovski* sailed with her sirens blaring. We tried to lay our hands on anything that would make a large enough wail in return. The tractor horn just squeaked and was quickly abandoned. The fire siren made a more respectable claxon.

On the Monday morning the weather was poor again so I was unable to return to Glacier Col but worked in the lab instead. Bob, a biologist, walked over to Maiviken, a small cove around the headland from the base, and discovered that the crew of the *Ostrovski* had broken into the hut over there and stolen the emergency rations.

The next day we had been challenged to a football match by the crew of the *Professor Bugoski*, a Russian trawler which had arrived on Monday morning followed shortly by a Polish vessel. Apparently *Ostrovski* had told *Bugoski* that they had beaten us 3–0, whereas in reality it was only 2–1. The base team trotted out onto the pitch, smartly turned out in black and white striped kit. We lined up along the half way line and faced a line of our opponents who wore any kit they could find. Both teams exchanged club pennants, just like in a proper international match. What is more, the entire crew of the Polish ship had come ashore and added to those from the Russian trawler to make a crowd of more than sixty. We had a Polish referee who kept good control of the game and we soundly beat our Russian opponents 3–0. Each time we scored the Poles politely but very quietly applauded but the Russians looked as grim faced as ever. As far as we were concerned that made the scores, England 4, Russia 2 on aggregate.

During the next two weeks I went up to Glacier Col with a number of people and completed most of my work. I was relatively pleased that the weather had been fairly kind all in all. My remaining task was to write a report about the work.

One of the aspects of the base I found most memorable was the generally convivial atmosphere there. That was not to say that there were no arguments. There were several real charactgers on base. There was Frank the base doctor who was studying syphyllis in seals as part of a research programme into why sealers were infected by the disease in their hands, an ailment known as 'seal finger'. There was a Mancunian called Pete who seemed to think that the more loudly he talked the more people would listen. He was wrong. And then there was Bob, alias 'Headcase'. He had been a customs official in Australia and had spent sometime in India in miscellaneous pursuits. He behaved as if he had just returned from the Raj at the turn of the century. One Saturday evening Bob was sitting at the bar after dinner, paralytic, with his white pith helmet on his head, when suddenly he straightened up, took a deep breath and said in a stentorian and very British way: 'When I was in India . . . ' At the same instant he twirled his moustache, keeled over backwards and fell in a drunken stupor onto the floor.

The other truly memorable aspect of my stay on South Georgia was the little Lutheran Church.

13: The Tonsberg Bells

The Lutheran Church at Grytviken was the only brightly decorated building on the station, its white walls and steeple making it stand out amidst all the rusty old remains of the whaling station. The front porch of the church consisted of an arched roof covering steps up both of its sides onto an area behind wooden bars. The main door opened directly beneath the squat square tower on which was a steep pyramidal steeple crowned with a cross. The steeple housed the belfry whose outward appearance was of louvred windows on each side of the tower. The bells themselves had been specially cast in 1912 in the famous foundry in Tonsberg in Norway. Their sound was delightful as it echoed around the cove and could be heard clearly from King Edward Point. The main body of the church was rectangular but at the far end was an L-shaped extension which housed the Pastor's vestry and a library of Norwegian books, many of which were still on the shelves when I visited. The dust was thick on the covers and the pages unread for many years.

The main part of the church housed ten rows of light wood pews either side of a wide central aisle which led to the altar area. On the right as one approached the front was a pulpit complete with its bishop-red lectern cloth. To the left of the aisle hung the vestments of the last incumbent. Over the white cassock was a crimson drape on which a goblet in a halo was embroidered in silver thread. On a raised dais behind a low semicircular rail with kneeling pads for the receipt of communion was the altar itself which was entirely plain and was draped in a simple white linen. Two large candles in equally large holders guarded either end of the altar. In the middle was an unadorned cross with two small pots of moss either side of it. The moss was the only plant that could be found to dress the altar, there being no suitable flowering plants on the islands. At the back of the altar was a silver piece on which the words of Matthew 11.28 were written in Norwegian: 'Kom til meg alle i som straever og har det tungt jeg vil give eder hvil' ('Come to me, all of you who are tired of carrying heavy loads, and I will give you rest.') What an apt verse considering the kind of life that those men and their families had at the turn of the century. How hard was their burden to survive in the long cold nights during winter bringing up small children. That verse must have brought great solace to them. What truths were contained in that text, if only people had taken the time to stop and think of them. Christianity is not a crutch on which those who are ordinarily too weak to survive in life can lean. That verse though tells a different story for it does not say 'I will take away your burden' or 'I will make it lighter for you' or even 'I will give you greater strength to be able to cope' but 'I will give you rest.' Overtired people often could not see problems in their real light and so the difficulties seemed even greater. If we can stop for a while, and rest and look at the problem when refreshed, then we would be able to cope more easily. God was not saying that he would do everything for us, but that the solution to our problems involved us in doing something to help ourselves. At the back of the church to the right of the main entrance was the organ which was still functional. Frank, the Base doctor, used to play it occasionally. To power it the organist had to peddle like mad as the bellows were foot operated.

Frank was keen to try to stop the church building from falling into disrepair. I tried to give him a hand when I could. Easter Sunday was one such occasion. We tried to paint as much of the outside of the building as we could. We were busy outside, so we burned two candles inside on the altar, more as a gesture than as part of any ritual. It seemed fitting that there should be something to commemorate Easter even if we were unable to hold a service there. When we had finished the painting I went inside and in my grubby clothes knelt at the altar rail by myself and read the text. Those few moments were some of the most precious of my entire Antarctic voyage and I wished that I could have spent longer there. It was so good to be in a church where I could spend time in meditation and quiet contemplation and prayer without the distractions of wayward vicars.

As we had missed holding a service on Easter Sunday it was decided that one should be held the following weekend. Frank did not feel happy at conducting the service and so it fell to my lot to do it. On the Saturday I went over to the church and tried to find the hymn books in order to choose some hymns which the organist could play and which had a message consistent with what I wanted to say in my brief sermon.

On the Sunday morning I walked the three quarters of a mile along the beach to find Andy, an ionosphericist*, who was to play the organ, locked out and standing by the porch. Frank was nowhere to be seen and he had the keys. I rushed back along the beach, dodged the three fur seals and arrived somewhat out of breath at Shack House and found Frank. It was only fifteen minutes before the service was due to start so we raced back to the church to find our congregation waiting outside. Not an auspicious start to the service. Within ten minutes our organist was installed and playing away, the congregation helped remove some ladders from across the pews so that they could sit down and someone rang the two church bells loudly and vigorously while I prepared myself in the pulpit. All was ready and so began the first service since a candlelit Christmas service eighteen months before. I spoke for longer than I had intended and went on for forty minutes. However, it did mean that Bob, who had timed his walk over to the church in order to miss the service, arrived too early and came in before I had finished so he had to sit through the last point of my sermon, a general hymn, a final prayer and the benediction. For Bob, a confirmed orthodox atheist, to have to sit through all that was quite a feat but he did so quietly. The subject of my sermon was 'The claims of Christ', a subject big enough for a dozen sermons. Like a true Baptist, I had three points to my talk: the prophecies concerning the advent and life of Christ, the historicity of Christ, and His claims in relation to the proofs of the resurrection – was he a madman, prophet, political leader, actor or the Son of God? We had seven intentional members of the congregation (including me) and Bob. When it was all over, I was delighted when several folk said that they had appreciated the service. To me that was great encouragement and made all the preparation worthwhile, although it would have been worthwhile even if no one had said anything.

After lunch I returned to the church as we were having a small party to celebrate the reopening of the church for the purpose for which it was built. The party was not very successful. One or two people showed no respect for the place at all, walking down the aisle shouting 'Where's the booze, then?' and bouncing a football as they went.

Following the success of the first service, we decided to hold another one the following Sunday. As *Bransfield* was due in then, more people might wish to attend and therefore we considered taking the opportunity to hold a communion service. There was no record as to when the last one of those had been held there, but I suspected that it was a matter of many years. If the ship did arrive, then I would have access to some of my books and they would be a great help in my preparation.

As I prepared for the service on what was to be my last Saturday on base, I felt sad. In the short time I had been on the island I had grown very fond of it and I almost felt loath to have to leave. I found such a sense of peace there, not necessarily the kind of peace that one associates with peace and quiet, but rather, an inner peace that I found very difficult to put into words. There was something special for me there, and the focus of it was that small Lutheran church. Perhaps it was that by having to prepare for the services, I had to prepare myself first. As I had been going through spiritually lean times that rededication was no bad thing. I felt far closer to God then than I had done at any other time on the voyage, before and after. It was as if the special thing about that island was that I had come closer to God there, and the closer one was to God, the nearer one was to heaven.

The disadvantage of having the communion service in the morning after the last night on base, was that many Fids overindulged themselves in alcohol the night before and so did not get up in time for the service, a fact for which many apologised. Nevertheless, I was surprised at how many attended; eleven of us in all, including a couple from the ship. None of us knew the tune to the first hymn so we sang it to one that we did know and that fitted. The service proceeded as planned and I spoke for the time that I had expected rather than overshooting like the previous Sunday. For my talk I chose the theme of 'The church of Christ – its foundation and building material'. I thanked the Lord that people commented, not just that they had enjoyed the service, but that they had been uplifted by it, which meant a great deal to me.

I was surprised, however, at the people who attended the two Sunday services. Some of them I would never have guessed were interested in Christianity. We had had a real cross section of professions; there was a doctor, an ionosphericist, a launchman, a builder, a painter/decorator, a terrestrial biologist (by accident, Bob), and myself, a glaciologist. Their professions were not my concern although it was good to see such a spread. Some of them were very heavy drinkers and swore a great deal. It was as if their weekly behaviour was permitted to be different from their Sunday behaviour; if they went to a service that absolved them of their week's misdoing. It relegated Christianity into a superstition. They might have well said 'touch wood'. But I felt that my feelings towards those men, perhaps outwardly judgemental, were wrong. Who was I to make comment on them? 'Let he who is without sin cast the first stone' said Jesus (John 8.7). Yet how often we do in our neat little churches. 'We don't want people like that in our church!' It was as if they were talking about membership of a golf club. The trouble with the church, as I saw it then, was that we wanted it to be filled with people that were like us, ordinary decent folk. Robbers, murderers, prostitutes, tramps, the long-term unemployed, drug addicts, the church was not for them, surely? Yet when Christ was born in Bethlehem, there were two sets of people who came to adore him. One was the three Magi from the east, probably the equivalent of university professors; the other was a group of shepherds out in the fields. They represented the lowliest of the whole of that society. They were too unclean to stay inside the confines of villages, their status was so low. Yet they were there first at the manger. Surely that was a message for us in that Christ came to this world for everyone, irrespective of their skin colour, their physical well being, their profession or social status, or even of their behaviour in society. No one was excluded and that is was as true now as it was two thousand years ago. The church of the twentieth century was there to help all people, especially those in need. A sign of the spiritual commitment of a church was, I felt, not just that there was standing room only at Sunday services, or that there was a thriving mid-week Bible study, but that the members of that church were actively engaged in practical Christianity. So often we could be so busy going to church meetings that we had no time to help those who needed us just to sit and be with them, not saying anything but being prepared to listen and to help in real terms. No longer muttering patronising 'God bless you' and putting a penny in the blind beggar's tin, but being a real help for the true needs of the individual. Drug abuse was on the increase, especially amongst schoolchildren, and desperately needed to be eradicated. To wean people off the drugs could be done in a fortnight; solving the problems of the addicts that sent them onto drugs in the first place could take years. It was the matter to which Christians should have been addressing themselves, as well as the immediate drugs problem. The church in the West was so weak and its ministry so cold and uncaring. It reminded me of a Hungarian minister, who was pastor of a prohibited underground church behind the Iron Curtain, who visited England. After a few weeks he longed for the fellowship of his home church. Despite the oppression and the fear of arrest and detention, his home church was alive. Its members needed to live by real faith in order to survive under their atheistic political regime. Of the British church, he said that it was not hot, it was not even lukewarm, but it was stone cold and totally ineffective. Perhaps if the church was forced underground in the west it might do more good than the total freedom that we had at that time. For we have the freedom to do nothing with our churches, we have the freedom to backslide in our communities. Where was the real commitment to Christ? In some places there were signs that there was a spark of life and that in the future the fire would be kindled. What was commitment? Attending church and its meetings? No. Real commitment was nicely explained by someone who said that we ought to consider a dish of egg and bacon. The chicken was involved but the pig was committed.

In all my thinking about the services that we had enjoyed at that little Lutheran church, I just hoped that something of what had been said had gone deep into people's hearts and minds. I could only have left them in God's hands for so often we could sow the seed but not be involved in the harvest.

Seed sowing was also what I hoped the redecorated church would do for visitors, especially from behind the Iron Curtain, like those Soviet and Polish seamen and women. For those occasional visitors to that historic building I left a pile of *The four Spiritual Laws,* copies of the Bible and of the New Testament, and also of *The Cross and the Switchblade* all in both Russian and Polish.

The communion service was my last task on the island, but in the afternoon there was to be a final football match between the ship and the base teams. I played for the ship this time and we won by two goals to one. That evening was the last one on the island for some of us. I was leaving after almost a month there, whereas several of my colleagues were going after two and a half years. To celebrate we had a spectacular feast of which the London Ritz would have been proud. The amount of food there was almost obscene, especially when millions of people were starving to death. Such thoughts were far from most people's minds and everyone had a good time and it was a fitting climax for most people. For me, the climax had been the communion service. After lunch that Sunday, I took all my kit aboard the ship. I had had my last night on the island, thereafter I was to stay on *Bransfield* until we reached Southampton some four weeks later.

On the Monday morning base personnel came on board and we said our farewells. Those staying on the island disembarked and stood on the jetty and, as the ship loosed her lines and edged away, we bombarded those ashore with flour bombs. They retaliated by turning a fire hose on to us but it was not powerful enough and the wind was in the wrong direction and so they ended up becoming soaked. Gradually the whaling station and then King Edward Cove grew distant as we steamed into Cumberland Bay and then northwards out into the open ocean.

14: Homecoming

The first four days of our journey north were spent on rough seas. Little was done on board except eat, stay on one's bunk and sleep. As time progressed so the weather improved, becoming increasingly hot as we sailed closer to Brazil and Rio.

Our first sight of Rio was of the mountains around the city which appeared as dark clouds. We could already smell the heady woody scent of the rain forest. As we approached Janeiro Bay, the famous Sugarloaf Mountain loomed high on our port side. Several Brazilian Navy vessels steamed out past us dipping their ensigns as they went. We could make out the distinctive figure of the statue of Christ with his outstretched arms in permanent welcome, high on one of the rocky peaks overlooking the city.

We docked soon after 10 am. It was hot and very humid. A massive nine-mile long bridge which spanned Janeiro Bay was lost in the haze.

Within minutes of docking, customs and immigration officers came aboard closely followed by our port agents who brought with them local currency and mail. The latter was quickly distributed and I received a healthy sized pile of letters – seven from my parents, one from my sister and her family and a long one from Sue, plus a large envelope of official blurb from my boss. I read everything very hastily, collected my local currency from the Fourth Officer, then went ashore to explore Rio.

The next day a large group of us made our way up towards Corcovado, where the enormous statue of Christ was situated. We had to travel the last part of the trip by minibuses as our coach was too large to ascend the steep tortuous road to the foot of the statue. Finally there was a climb of 200 or more steps to the foot of the monument. The Christ figure was swathed in swirling clouds which cleared momentarily just long enough to take a photograph or two. The view from the balustrade around the statue was fantastic. The whole city of Rio sprawled before us like a carpet. We could easily make out Sugarloaf Mountain and the famous beaches of Copacobana, Ipanema, Leblon and Flamengo, the first of which we were to visit next after refreshments. The beach was surprisingly empty even though the sun was hot and the sea warm. The following five days were spent shopping, sightseeing and generally having a very pleasant time.

On our last evening in Rio a group of us went to one of the less salubrious night clubs. As soon as we entered we were accosted by prostitutes. I was being pestered by one woman who spoke passable English. Eventually I gave her 100 cruseiros for her to take a taxi home.

A few moments later one of the most attractive of the women I had seen asked me to dance. At first I was reluctant but then agreed. She tried to teach me the samba or rather a disco version of it. Anna was of Swedish parentage, blonde and petite. She kept muttering some very flattering things to me as we danced. I knew what she was trying to do and I had to keep telling myself that she said the same things to every bloke she met. When she danced a short while with a girl friend of hers, I took the chance to slip away. She soon realised and chased after me, but I headed for the ship, pleased that I had not given in to temptation. I had thoroughly enjoyed my last evening in Rio. However, I had a nagging thought in my mind I had played Anna at her own game, but deep inside it made me feel sad. I later learned from a colleague that he had seen her sitting on a bench not far from where I had left her, crying. It really mixed me up. On the one hand I knew she was a prostitute and that I had done the right thing in leaving her, on the other, I had this mental picture of an attractive woman left all alone, sobbing, still a human being, still a person. Perhaps her isolation was far worse than any I had experienced in Antarctica. At least mine was temporary – I was going home to family and friends. For her, what release would there be? I also felt conflict because as a Christian I knew I should not even have gone into bars like that or sat or danced with those women, but I was subject to all the temptations that everyone else was. Had I done wrong? I really did not know. I remembered how Christ himself had mingled with prostitutes and had not judged them but had said that they, like tax collectors, if they accepted Him as Lord, would go into the Kingdom of Heaven ahead of the self-righteous Pharisees, the guardians of Jewish religious law (Matthew 21, verse 31). Was I being Pharisaical? I did not know and I could not decide what I ought to have done in the circumstances. It was history now, but I had learned a lesson. I had also learned a lot about myself and had identified more weaknesses. The swirl of ideas did not polarise into right and wrong but kept spinning until I went to sleep in my pit.

At lunch time next day *Bransfield's* siren blared, the engines throbbed and the water astern churned as the ship moved from the quayside and away from Rio. Gradually, the city faded into the afternoon heat haze. A post-Rio lethargy started to set in. As the days passed, people became increasingly keen to return to England. Base support staff and GAs technically ceased to be employed by BAS on the day of arrival in the United Kingdom so they had no jobs to which to return and this played on some of them. For research staff, our biggest problem was to find accommodation in Cambridge. Yet despite these rather negative aspects of our return, most people were pleased to be going back.

On our sixth day out from Rio, we held the traditional Crossing the Line ceremony to celebrate passing over the Equator. Although I had flown south that did not disqualify me from being initiated according to the time-honoured custom by Neptune himself. Those of us who had never sailed across the line before were told to prepare some form of entertainment with which to amuse Neptune's followers or else some dreadful lurgy would befall us. Jerry, fellow glaciologist, and I were both in the same situation so we decided to combine our efforts.

After dinner, people started to congregate on the helideck which had been rigged with coloured lights and arc lamps and which looked very decorative. For those of us about to be anointed by Neptune they were hours of trepidation in anticipation of what was to follow. At 9.15 pm, the proceedings were called to order and Jerry and I were the first initiates to perform. The act was that Jerry should lather his face and shave. The trick was that I was behind Jerry with my arms doing the shaving but with me not being able to see what I was doing. As far as the audience was concerned they could only see Jerry with his towel around his shoulders and a pair of somewhat uncoordinated arms. Consequently, the lather went in his eyes, ears, over his nose and occasionally where it was supposed to go. Greater hilarity (for the audience; panic for Jerry) was when I found the razor and tried to apply it. All went very well – the audience enjoyed it, Jerry survived without me drawing his blood and we had pleased Neptune. As we finished a hose with cold sea water was turned on us plus a spray of beer from shaken beer cans. Eventually we were awarded our Crossing the Line Certificate duly signed by the ship's captain and, of course, Neptune himself. Other initiates followed us, one sang a song, another played the guitar and sang, someone did some gymnastics and yoga. One of the stewards stoically played his violin even though a hosepipe had been stuck down his trousers and turned full on. One potential initiate refused to oblige and so Neptune's wrath was kindled. Once he was caught he had the slops bucket tipped over him and down inside his trousers, plus a bucket full of a special concoction made up for the occasion which was a vivid green slime and was similarly administered to the culprit.

The closer we were to home, the more thoughts turned to family and friends and the more noticeable it was that folk were becoming tensed up about our imminent arrival at Southampton. People were becoming far less tolerant of each other over trivial matters; for instance, in the deck quoits tournament, several Fids almost came to blows over the interpretation of a minor rule. It had been known for people to have fist fights over such apparently trivial matters such as the way to hold a fork!

Our route took us past the giant sea cliffs of Madeira, though the bay of Biscay, to the English Channel. Here, the number of ships we encountered increased markedly. We also sailed quite close to several drilling platforms, and were greeted a short while later by an RAF Nimrod from Coastal Command. The plane made four low passes around us and on the last one dipped its wings as a welcome and then departed. It was a splendid sight. Entry to the English Channel was celebrated with the traditional fancy dress party known as 'Channel Night'. It was a very amusing evening with most people turning up in a great variety of custumes. I went as a Roman Centurion, Jerry went as Mrs Mop, the captain went as a Lieutenant in the Royal Navy Reserve (which he was anyway), the junior most deck boy went as the captain of the *Bransfield*; there was someone as a yellow submarine, Poof in Boots, a Zulu warrior, a Harlequin, various famous pop stars, a clown, a hoolahoola dancer, an Arab, and so on. Part of the way through the festivities, the lighthouse at Prawle Point on the south-east corner of Devon was sighted to great cheers from the party goers. When I went to bed, I glanced at the northern skyline and could make out the glow of lights from towns along the south coast of England. Nearly home!

At breakfast the next morning, we were able to look out at the coast of the Isle of Wight as we slowly sailed towards Southampton. As we made our final approach to berth we could see a large crowd of people on the quayside waving and cheering. Tension on board was terrific, with some people really excited at seeing folk again whilst others were quite fearful at the prospect. Some voiced worries that their girlfriends might have changed for the worse since they last saw each other, others had no one to meet them and just wanted to get away as quickly as possible. Friends had swapped addresses to be able to keep in contact if they were not to be based at BAS headquarters in Cambridge. It was a time when the people about whom Fids had told stories would appear in the flesh. The fantasies that some men talked about would not appear quite so marvellous in reality. The Fid uniform of checked shirt and grey moleskin trousers was nowhere to be seen. In its place was more fashionable attire, jackets and ties which had not seen the light of day for months, freshly ironed cotton shirts, pressed trousers and polished shoes. As the ship neared the last few yards to the quayside, faces within the waiting crowd became identifiable. 'There's my Jimmy!' cried one woman loudly, pointint to the Fid-deck rail lined with dozens of men, any one of whom could have been her 'Jimmy'. 'Oh God, there she is!' bemoaned one Fid, a builder from Rothera. 'She looks awful!' He walked dejectedly into the Fiddery muttering 'What am I going to do? I wrote her some very encouraging letters and even mentioned getting married. But look at her, she's got fat!' I searched the quayside and saw no familiar faces. I could not stand peering over the side to pick out relatives so I retired to my cabin and waited there.

Once moored alongside, customs officials were soon

aboard and we had the rigmarole of declaring goods and souvenirs. The customs men were very good and we were quickly cleared, although one Fid who had made a beautiful scale model of a muskeg had to pay fifty pounds import duty on it as the customs man was not convinced that it had been made out of scrap metal.

As soon as the customs were through, the horde of waiting relatives and friends were unleashed to board the ship. Never had the ship been so crowded as it was then. There seemed to be hardly any room to breathe for all the fur coats and fancy hairstyles and posh hats filling up the corridors. I took respite in my cabin until folk had dispersed a little more evenly around the Fid-deck. After a short wait I went out in the fray and saw my mother and sister who had driven over from Cornwall to meet me. Once contact had been made it was great to see them again. I had half-hoped that perhaps Sue would have come down from London to meet the ship but I was not surprised that she was not there. The final few minutes on board *Bransfield* were a blur. It was hard to say cheerio to some Fids as firm friendships had been made and there was no telling when folk would meet again. One by one, the families having claimed their Fids, they filed off the ship clutching masses of clatch which they endeavoured to pack into cars which suddenly seemed far too small to cope.

I felt that I wanted to leave as quickly as possible, to get away from the crowd of people more than anything, just to have some space in which to think. I did not say much at first as we drove out of the city towards the south-west. There was so much to take in, and so quickly. There were women again, and traffic, green fields and trees. How we had missed trees! We stopped off at a pub for lunch and my first shock was the price of a drink! Dealing with real money seemed strange – the coins and notes in Rio had been more like play cash than hard currency. As we drove west, my mother turned to me and asked, 'Well, then.

What's it feel like to be back?' How could I answer? On the one hand it felt great, on the other, I was in a daze as it seemed as if I had just been transported from a different planet back to Earth.

15: The Aftermath

Through my travels to and from Antarctica I had found God to be present wherever I was and in whatever I was doing. Any isolation I might have felt was not from Him deserting me, but from me distancing myself from Him by inserting between us a barrier of sin. My voyage had enabled me to identify some of my inner problems and to start to find solutions with Christ's help. Life has not been any more difficult or easier than before. At least now I know that, as long as I am doing God's will, He will give me the means to succeed. God's will might mean a difficult life, but by working for Him I know I am doing the right thing. At times I have found it hard to find out what I should be doing, but I have found that God honours the sincerity of those who seek.

The spiritual lessons I had learnt over my six-month trip enabled me to cope once I was back in England. The first few days at home seemed strange but before long, it was almost as if I had never been away. It was a matter of re-acclimatising. However, emotionally, it was a more protracted easing back into society. One phenomenon of which returning Fids have to be aware is 'emotional rebound'. During the time of separation from a loved one the attractiveness of the partner is heightened almost to the point of fantasy, and any less desirable aspects of the person are suppressed. Consequently over a period of time, be it six months or two years, the Fid can believe his mental picture of his girlfriend and respond to that rather than to the real person. The tangible effect of this is the increasing endearment expressed in a Fid's letters to his girlfriend. The extreme of this is that the Fid falls in love with the concept of an attractive girlfriend, rather than with the reality of the person concerned. This can lead to considerable disappointment on both sides upon the return of the Fid. His girlfriend has a nigh on impossible task of living up to his mental picture of what she should be like, and this causes increased tensions and has been the final straw for many relationships, marriages included.

On the other hand, emotional rebound can be the opposite. If the Fid did not have a girlfriend over the period of his Antarctic tour, his separation from women could lead him to fall head over heels with the first woman who shows an interest in him, however small. Marriages based on this are also doomed.

Upon my return I had to sort out my relationship with Sue. Where was it going? It turned out that I had been suffering from the first type of Antarctic emotional rebound. I had been reading far more into Sue's letters than was really there. I had misinterpreted Sue's gestures of friendship as implying a greater fondness of me. Our friendship continued after my return, but she very kindly and gently put me in my place. We remained good friends, but our relationship stayed at that. In time I came to realise that if two people were to become serious about each other they needed to see one another very frequently. With Sue in London and me in Cambridge it was not going to flourish; we both accepted that. In time, I realised the next stage of God's plan for me when I met Moira in Cambridge. About a year after my return from Antarctica we were engaged, and the following Christmas, we were married.

Given the opportunity to go south again, would I? Without hesitation, yes!

Glossary

All the terms which have been asterisked within this book appear in this glossary. Words which are of Fid derivation or adaption are marked (F). The etymology of other words is either unclear or can be obtained from reference works such as dictionaries.

Alpha Quebec – call sign for one of the Twin Otter aircraft.

Alpha Whiskey – call sign for one of the Twin Otter aircraft.

Barchan – crescentic shaped sand or snow dune.

Bergschrund – deep crevasse in a glacier adjacent to the junction between a steep rock wall and the ice below.

Bergy Bits – fragments of icebergs but which are larger than growlers, eg about the size of an ordinary house.

Biscuit (F) – affectionate name given to RRS *John Biscoe*.

Bodge (F) – temporary solution. Normally badly or amateurishly rectified, hence a 'Fid bodge job'.

Bog Chisel (F) – flat bladed tool with a 5 ft long handle used for probing for crevasses.

Boot (F) – verb equivalent to 'to be cross', hence to be boot.

Brash Ice – small fragments and floes of ice freely floating in water.

Brantub (F) – affectionate name given to RRS *Bransfield*.

Breccia – angular fragments of rock naturally cemented or fused together to form a coherent unit.

Ching (F) – verb to part with one's girlfriend, hence to ching or be chinged. Also 'Ching Award' for the most significant break-up of a season, eg by a fiancée or wife.

Clatch (F) – baggage taken on a journey; sometimes used in a derogatory sense to imply excessive and unnecessary gear.

Contrast – describes the contrast between the ground and the sky and the degree of ease with which ground features such as surface snow roughness can be distinguished. Poor contrast means that even major ice cliffs can be virtually invisible.

Deadman – a flat plate attached to a cable or rope and used in mountaineering as an anchor.

Depot (F) – verb 'to depot' something is to dump or store equipment in a temporary cache, hence a stranded sledge could have been depoted (pronounced 'dep-owed').

Dingle (F) – fine weather, hence a 'dingle day' and 'it's dingle'.

'Doo – abbreviation of skidoo, a motorised toboggan. The verb 'to 'doo' means to travel by skidoo, eg a Fid 'dooed over to Mount . . .

Ellie (F) – abbreviation for elephant seal.

Encumbrance (F) – affectionately derogatory name given to HMS *Endurance*, the Royal Navy ice patrol vessel.

Fast Ice – sea ice frozen fast to shore.

FID (F) – in the early days, the name of the organisation was Falkland Islands Dependencies Survey (FIDS). The men who served on the bases called themselves 'Fids' and on their return home after leaving the survey 'ex-Fids'. Inexperienced men on their first season south were called 'Fidlets'. Staff employed on permanent contracts were known as Perma-Fids and, if senior in rank, 'Super-Fids'.

The unique and distinctive terminology used by Fids has the name 'Fid-ese'.

Fiddery (F) – The mess room on base or ship used exclusively by Fids. On board ship, 'Super-Fids' had use of their own 'Super-Fiddery'.

Flensing Plan – flat area in a whaling station on which the mammal's carcase is dismembered or flensed.

Furkle (F) – to tweak or fiddle with a machine or instrument, eg a temperamental carburettor would be furkled to make it work.

Gash – naval term for rubbish; wet gash is the slops and waste food, dry gash is paper rubbish. To be on 'gash' is to be responsible for housework, washing up etc, hence a 'gashman' is a Fid on gash duty.

Goodies (F) – usually food but may include any item considered to be a luxury over and above normal issue, hence a 'goodies box', a manfood box which contains goodies.

Goon Show (F) – radio get-together on the air.

Growler – fragments of ice usually from icebergs, about the size of a family car, which is free floating, and when in a sea swell with brash ice makes noises which evidently resemble low growls.

Ice Piedmont – lobate part of a land-based glacier, normally its snout.

Ice Shelf – a large featureless flat expanse of glacier ice which has gone afloat.

Ionosphericist – a scientist who studies the part of the upper atmosphere called the ionosphere.

Jolly (F) – a trip or holiday for fun and recreation. Also, a 'jolly-merchant' is one who takes a reputedly excessive number of jollies and perhaps tries to justify them as being for official purposes; used in a derogatory manner.

Jumar – clamp-like device to enable a climber to ascend a rope.

Karabina – metal ring used in mountaineering.

Katabatic Wind – a wind caused by cold air flowing downhill by virtue of being denser than the lower warmer air; common in glacierised areas.

Manfood (F) – food rations for field work for one man for normally ten days.

Mank (F) – adjective for overcast or cloudy, hence a 'manky sky' or as a noun for clouds, hence 'mank down to the ground' (very low cloud).

Meat Bar (F) – dehydrated compressed cooked meat in bar form.

'Men' (F) – 'the Men', ie the huskies.

Metamorphic Rock – rock which has been recrystallised by the action of temperature and/or pressure in the solid state, eg slate.

Muffin (F) – girlfriend.

Muskeg – a type of tractor with caterpillar tracks, also called a 'keg'.

Nunatak – Eskimo word for a rock peak entirely surrounded by ice.

Onitsuka – Japanese make of thermally insulated sledging boot.

P-Bag (F) – a weather-proofed canvas bag used to contain a Fid's sleeping bag, sheepskin, bivouac bag, spare clothes and small personal items, and which is supposed to accompany him on all trips away from base or camp.

Perma-Fid (F) – see under 'Fid'.

Pit – naval term for bed or sleeping bag.

Prussik Loop – a small loop of strong but small diameter rope which can be used to provide friction on another rope and be used like a jumar, for example.

Pup-Tent – a small single-skinned ridge tent for two people.

Radio Sched (F) – scheduled radio contact between base/ship and field parties etc.

Rev (F) – verb to rush around with a sense of urgency; a 'rev-merchant' is a Fid who unnecessarily and too frequently revs.

Scradge (F) – food or meals, hence a 'scradge mechanic' is a cook and a 'scradge palace' is a dining room.

Scrub-Out – general weekly clean up involving all Fids on base or ship.

Seracs – unstable towers or pinnacles of glacier ice formed in an icefall of a glacier, and highly dangerous.

Sledge Biscuit (F) – a type of dry biscuit provided in sledging rations.

Sledge Wheel (F) – a single bicycle wheel which is towed from the back of a sledge or a skidoo, and which has a mileometer on it which is used to help in navigation by measuring the distance travelled.

Skidoo – a motorised toboggan, usually 640 cc engine capacity with drive provided via two caterpillar tracks and steering by one front ski to a motorbike handlebar; known as a 'doo.

Smokoh (F) – coffee or tea break.

Snowcat – a heavy duty tractor with an enclosed cabin, with four caterpillar tracks and specially designed for over snow travelling; also called a 'cat.

Twotter (F) – abbreviation of Twin Otter, a de Havilland twin-engined aircraft.

Witter (F) – chitchat, especially over the radio, hence 'to have a witter' or to 'witter with someone'.

82 Bravo – a navigation marker point at 82 degrees latitude south.

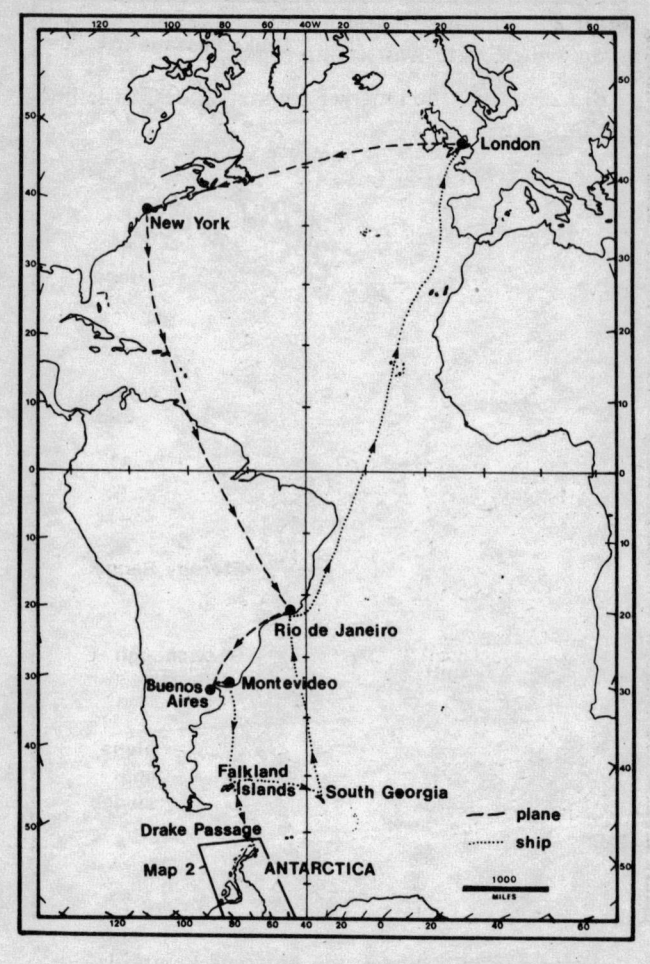

Approximate route taken to and from the Antarctic.

188

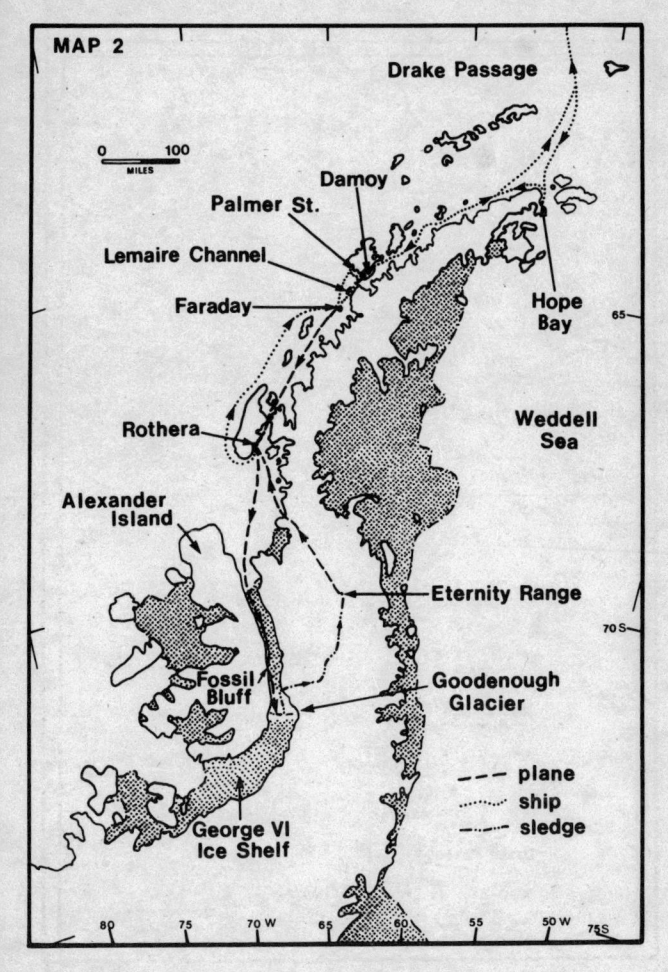

Routes taken whilst in the Antarctic Peninsula.

Other Marshall Pickering Paperbacks

FORGIVE AND RESTORE

Don Baker

When a member of God's family, in this case a loved pastor, goes seriously off the rails in his personal life, the questions looms large, What should the church do about it? Is it a matter for the church leadership only? Should the wayward member be asked to leave or just relieved of responsibility? What should the congregation be told?

This book is a remarkable account of how one church dealt with such a highly charged and emotional crisis. It records in honest detail the ebb and flow of hope and despair, uncertainty and humanity, and relying throughout on biblical principles, it picks its way through a tangled mess to find a place of healing and restoration again.

WHEN YOU PRAY

Reginald East

Spiritual renewal has awakened in many Christians a deeper longing to know God more intimately. Prayer is the place where we personally meet God, yet it is often treated simply as the means for making requests for our needs, and offering our stilted, dutiful thanks. In this practical guide to prayer, Reginald East shows how we can establish a prayer relationship with God which is both spiritually and emotionally satisfying. Through understanding God and ourselves better, prayer can truly become an encounter with God, where we relax into Him, enjoy Him, listen as well as talk to Him and adventure into discovering His heart of love.

If you wish to receive *regular information* about *new books*, please send your name and address to:

London Bible Warehouse
PO Box 123
Basingstoke
Hants RG23 7NL

Name _____

Address _____

_____

_____

_____

I am especially interested in:
- [ ] Biographies
- [ ] Fiction
- [ ] Christian living
- [ ] Issue related books
- [ ] Academic books
- [ ] Bible study aids
- [ ] Children's books
- [ ] Music
- [ ] Other subjects

P.S. If you have ideas for new Christian Books or other products, please write to us too!